The Modern L[
Teacher's Handbook

D1485207

Continuum Education Handbooks

A companion website to accompany this book is available online at: http://education.ramage.continuumbooks.com

Please type in the URL above to receive your unique password for access to the book's online resources.

If you experience any problems accessing the resources, please contact Continuum at: info@continuumbooks.com

Also available from Continuum

100+ Ideas for Teaching Languages, Nia Griffith
French in the Primary Classroom, Angela McLachlan
Getting the Buggers into Languages, Amanda Barton

The Modern Languages Teacher's Handbook

Gill Ramage

continuum

Continuum International Publishing Group

The Tower Building	80 Maiden Lane
11 York Road	Suite 704
London SE1 7NX	New York NY 10038

www.continuumbooks.com

British Library Cataloguing-in-Publication Data
A catalogue record for this book is available from the British Library.

ISBN: 978-1-4411-5860-4 (paperback)
      978-1-4411-3314-4 (ePub)
      978-1-4411-7797-1 (PDF)

Library of Congress Cataloging-in-Publication Data
Ramage, Gill.
  The modern languages teacher's handbook / Gill Ramage.
    p. cm. – (Continuum education handbooks)
  Includes bibliographical references and index.
  ISBN 978-1-4411-5860-4 – ISBN 978-1-4411-3314-4 –
  ISBN 978-1-4411-7797-1 1. Language and languages – Study and teaching.
  2. Language and languages – Handbooks, manuals, etc.   I. Title.
  P53.R36 2012
  418.0071–dc23

                                                    2011047616

Typeset by Newgen Imaging Systems Pvt Ltd, Chennai, India
Printed and bound in India

For Pete, Lynn and Alison, and my parents

Contents

Acknowledgements

The ideas of a range of teachers and fellow modern languages professionals have helped to inform this book: thanks to them for their valuable insights over the years. A list of publications and websites I have found useful is at the back of this book.

Particular thanks to my friend and mentor, Judith Buchanan; my inspirational former colleagues Marina Dixon and Lara Townsend; and that excellent group of people, the modern languages teachers of Suffolk. I am grateful to Suffolk County Council for permission to reproduce a range of material.

Introduction

Teaching modern languages can be fulfilling, frustrating, exhilarating, exhausting, entrancing, tedious or all of the above.

Whether you are a newly qualified teacher, a practising teacher, head of a modern languages department or considering teaching modern languages as a career, the following chapters aim to equip you well for teaching languages in the twenty-first century.

This handbook will give you an overview of how best to organize yourself and your teaching in order to get the best out of your students. It is a practical guide, based on years of experience and current best practice. Each chapter focuses on a key area of language teaching and gives you advice on how to tackle it successfully while keeping yourself sane. Although it is artificial to focus on each of the four language skills separately, chapters have been organized in this way for clarity's sake. You will not find separate chapters on teaching lower attainers or gifted and talented students: instead, ideas for differentiation, supporting and challenging students are included within chapters. Similarly, as new technologies are so integral to learning and teaching, chapters include how to use information and communication technology (ICT) to enhance each aspect of your work.

Although the exemplification in this book is mainly though French and German examples, the ideas and principles of course apply to whatever language you may be teaching, be that Spanish or Polish, Chinese or Gaelic.

If you want to develop your teaching further, there is a list of publications and websites at the back of this book. Many exciting modern languages practitioners today generously share their ideas and resources through their own websites or blogs. Time spent investigating these ideas and sharing your own via cyberspace can be an excellent source of continued professional development.

Lastly, as with all things in life, there is not one 'correct' way of teaching modern languages. Nevertheless, there are certain key principles which you need to keep in mind, and these form the basis of this book.

What's the point of learning a language?

As a prospective or practising modern languages teacher, you are the living embodiment of what learning a language can mean. If you are an English native speaker, you have no doubt gathered a wealth of experience during your language learning career, including travelling and making bonds with people from other countries, which would have been impossible had you not been a speaker of *their* language. If you are a native speaker of the language you are teaching, then again, it is because of your skills in languages that you have ended up where you are today: living and working in another country and communicating on a daily basis with a whole new world of individuals.

Teaching a foreign language in the United Kingdom or any other English-speaking country can sometimes feel like an uphill struggle. As language teachers, at some stage, we will without doubt hear our students ask 'What's the point?' Learning a foreign language in the United Kingdom cannot really be compared with learning English in other countries: in many countries, learning English is seen as a necessity to get on in the world and young people are surrounded by English in magazines, adverts, TV and films, pop songs, computer games and the internet. For most of our students, the importance of learning a foreign language is not so obviously visible in their everyday lives. Yet, foreign language classes for adults are one of the most popular evening classes of all: how often might you hear a parent comment at parents' evening 'I wish I'd paid more attention in modern language lessons when I was at school.'?

We know what learning a language can bring to us as human beings, and as teachers, it is up to us to put this passion and enthusiasm for our subject over to our students. As a new entrant to the profession or an experienced teacher, you are working at a time when fewer older students are studying languages. Political influences on the curriculum continue to come and go, and things may change for the better. Nevertheless, our task remains that of convincing our students that learning another language is one of the most worthwhile things they can do.

Establishing your own rationale for teaching modern languages

It is important to have a clear rationale in your own mind for the teaching of modern languages in general, and the language or languages you teach in particular. If this is clear to you, it will be easier to put this across to your students in both what you do and the way you do it. Your particular rationale will depend on your own views and the setting you are teaching in.

★ *Languages for intercultural understanding*

One of my favourite quotes about language learning is from Nelson Mandela:

> If you talk to a man in a language he understands, that goes to his head. If you talk to him in his language, that goes to his heart.

Curriculum materials in the United Kingdom, such as the *Primary Languages Framework* and the *Modern Foreign Languages Key Stage 3 Framework*, emphasize the key importance of intercultural understanding within modern languages, making it a strand of learning with equal weight to the functional skills of listening, speaking, reading and writing. Whether your school has students from many different cultural backgrounds or from one predominant background, being able to empathize with others and see things through their eyes is an important aspect of living in today's world. Through learning a new language, we can make all sorts of discoveries about another culture and improve our overall abilities to empathize and identify with others.

★ Languages for the world of work

Being able to speak and understand another language can open up immense opportunities for work, both abroad and in this country. Students do not need to be experts: being able to meet, greet and talk about a colleague's family in his or her own language can act as the cement in a working relationship. The National Centre for Language Teaching (CILT, formerly the National Centre for Languages, now part of CfBT Education Trust) and the website www.languageswork.org.uk produce a host of statistics, advice, resources and information on the importance of languages to industry. Ensure that you are well briefed on such opportunities so that you can tell students about them with conviction.

For post-16 students, having a proficient ability in a language can set them apart from the crowd and open the door to a range of university and career options. Furthermore, many universities in the United Kingdom offer students the chance to undertake part of their degree course abroad, even if they are not studying languages. The United Kingdom needs linguists, and our students need to know this. Students also need to understand that learning one language stands them in good stead to quickly pick up another.

★ Languages for leisure

Most travel from the United Kingdom is to Europe, and France and Spain are consistently among the countries most frequently visited by UK citizens. As you know, we can get so much more out of a holiday if we are able to communicate with the people there and really get involved with the culture. Students may well argue that English is commonly spoken in tourist resorts, but many people speak no English and, even if they do, it is much more polite (and fulfilling) to be able to speak in the language of the country you are visiting. Do your students know that 70 per cent of the world's population speak no English? (Source: CILT website, 2011.)

★ *Languages for life skills*

It can be frustrating when students ask what the point of their language lessons is because they are 'never going to go to France (or Spain/Japan) anyway', yet more often than not, they do not question why they are learning calculus or the atomic structure of nitrogen. Apart from the practical applications of languages (see above), it is important to be able to justify modern languages as a subject on the curriculum in its own right. For me, this is crucial and needs to be made explicit to students: even if they never set foot in the country whose language they are learning, the skills that they learn in the language classroom are ones which they can apply across all aspects of their lives, both in school and as adults.

Most obviously, students develop their general oral and literacy skills through learning another language. For example, they learn how to listen for gist and detail, how to skim and scan texts to find the information they need. They learn how to construct coherent pieces of writing and how to give presentations, speaking with confidence. All of these skills are transferable to their English work and to adult life.

Learning a language also involves the development of a range of thinking skills. Patterns play a huge part: the analysis of these patterns in order to pull out rules and then apply them in a logical way is a key skill in successful language learning. Learning how to make connections and apply patterns in language learning helps students to build up their generic thinking skills for application in other areas.

Finally, language learning is a social activity, with speaking and listening at its heart. Students can learn to work well with other people, in pairs and in groups. They can learn how to collaborate with each other and, literally, how to get along better with people.

To make sure that our language lessons enable students to develop all of these skills, we need outstanding lessons. If we are truly going to help students improve their life skills, our approach cannot be 'I'll tell you it, you repeat it, you copy it down, you learn it!'

Helping students to see the point

★ *The influence of languages in everyday life*

Help students to see that the languages they are learning are used every day in the real world by asking them to research where in the world the language is spoken, and by how many people. You may also like to find out more about languages spoken by students, parents and staff within the school so that students see the range of languages others use, even in their own locality. Students can be stunned to learn that their peers speak another language when they go home from school.

When students first start a new language, I like to ask them to look for things in their own household that are produced in countries where the language they are studying is spoken, such as foods, household products and cars, so that they can see the influence of other countries on their own daily lives. Ask them to look for examples of the foreign language which have been 'borrowed' by English, so that they can see how other languages have influenced their own.

★ *The world of work*

Ask students to search the internet and the press for jobs which require knowledge of the language they are studying. Make a display of job adverts which require some level of language ability.

In the classroom, think of workplace situations in the United Kingdom which you can use as scenarios for language use. If you are working on finding out about tourist attractions, turn the situation round so that students are not foreign tourists asking for leaflets in Germany, for example, but British tourist information centre workers answering questions from German tourists.

Within your General Certificate of Secondary Education (GCSE) or equivalent examination specification, you may well be given the opportunity to personalize the context for written or spoken work. Opt for exploring a work-related learning context to which your students will be able to relate. For example, use a local business as the context for an email to be written or a phone call conversation. You may also want to explore other qualifications which are specifically work related, for example, National Vocational Qualifications (NVQ) Language Units.

Links with local businesses that work with foreign clients are a good way of showing students the relevance of what they are learning. Classroom visits from former students who have gone on to use languages in their work, or from parents who use their language skills in their job, can help to motivate and inspire.

★ *Engagement through context*

Students need to see languages not just in a functional, practical way but also as an exciting school subject with interesting content. Thinking back to the past, I can remember asking many a 16-year-old GCSE candidates 'Do you have a pet?' or 'Can you describe your bedroom?' In short, the content of language lessons is not always appropriate to the maturity level of our students. An additional problem for students is that the modern languages teaching programme can sometimes seem like a constant recycling of the same thing: in the English system, potentially at least, students could learn to describe their family in primary school, then again at the start of secondary school, once more for their GCSE examination, and yet again when they look at relationships and family problems post-16.

It is true that content or topics are usually prescribed for examinations taken at (the specifications start at age 14) age 16 years and beyond. However, within these specifications, there is often scope for extended study on a topic selected by the school, teacher or student. For younger learners, the current national curriculum for England and Wales does not have any prescribed topics. Teachers are therefore free to use contexts and topics which motivate, engage and give scope for student creativity. Grammar, structures and the development of linguistic skills can be 'overlaid' over any topic. For example, a unit of work can be based around a foreign language film; a murder mystery story can be used as a context in which to focus on the imperfect tense ('What *were* you doing when the murder happened?'); a sports event (e.g. the World Cup or the Olympic Games) can form the basis of a whole unit of work. There is more on adopting such an approach in Chapter 2.

Borrowing subject matter from other subject areas provides a rich vein of contexts for language learning, although we need to make sure that the level of cognitive challenge is appropriate for learners of that age. This could involve, for example, looking at the work of an artist from the target language country, or linking language work on home and environment with geography work on the same topic area.

Content and Language Integrated Learning (CLIL) entails teaching another curriculum subject using the foreign language as the medium of communication. The emphasis is on the content of the other subject rather than on the foreign language, which in this scenario is a means to an end rather than the end itself. This sort of methodology, resulting from a whole school approach, requires expertise and planning but can have exciting results for both motivation and achievement.

★ *Engagement through intercultural understanding*

Building up intercultural understanding involves getting students to try to look through the eyes of speakers of different languages. Finding out about other countries and how things work there is as aspect of language learning which usually interests students. At the most basic level, they want to know what young people are like in that country and what they enjoy doing. So, for example, when you are working on a context such as school life, teach the topic content through a real school from the target language country. You can still use the 'generic' activities from your textbook for practice, but basing your work around a real school website, photos, subject descriptions and timetables will make your students that bit more interested.

Intercultural understanding of course goes beyond knowledge of facts about the target language country. When your students are learning about different aspects of culture, be sure to ask them to compare, contrast, discuss and evaluate as well. Try to be sure you do not reinforce stereotypical images yourself by recognizing diversity within the culture you are studying: not everybody has a croissant for breakfast in France, just as we do not all start every day with a fry-up.

★ *Flagging up the development of skills*

Ensuring that students see language learning as important to their overall development as thinkers is most effectively done through the way you present your lessons. Make the development of skills clear in the learning objectives you share with the students. Make sure you then deliver this through a series of planned activities so that students can see they are making progress. Make explicit when thinking skills and communication skills are being developed as part of the lesson and build in assessment so that students are rewarded for progress in these generic skills. Finally, through plenary sessions, ask students how the skills they have learned in their modern languages lesson can be applied to their other school subjects and to their everyday life in general.

Raising the profile of modern languages within the school

Sometimes it is not just the students who question the place of languages in the curriculum. Some headteachers and fellow colleagues do not believe that learning a language is relevant to all learners. This can lead to both practical difficulties, such as option blocks which do not encourage students to choose a language, and less overt messages being given to students that languages are not really that important anyway.

Battling against such a scenario is the job of the whole languages department, not any one teacher. Learning and teaching in the classroom needs to be your priority, but there is a range of other things you can do in order to keep the profile of modern languages high in the school as a whole. Do not attempt everything at once; prioritize, select and gradually build up profile-raising activities such as the following.

Celebrating success: Send postcards home (signed by the headteacher) when students do particularly well in your subject. Choose a language-related picture or design for your postcard. For each year group, you could also select a 'Linguist of the Month', displaying his or her photo with an explanation of why he or she has been selected. Be sure to reward students from across the ability spectrum. Make sure that the students are happy to be publicly recognized in this way.

Awarding certificates for progress: You can do this by following a formal scheme of assessment (such as Asset Languages) or by producing your own in-house certificates to mark achievement. Ask the headteacher to sign the certificates so that he or she is aware of successes in your department, and request a slot in assembly so that the certificates can be given out in a blaze of publicity.

Celebrating the European Day of Languages (26 September): Hold a series of events across the school. If you find the date comes around too quickly for you following the summer break, choose another day to designate as 'Languages Day', or, if you are feeling brave, have a 'Languages Week'. You can also celebrate national days or specific festivals with a link to the country whose language you are studying.

Labelling your school: With permission, label up rooms around the entire school in the language you are teaching so that staff and students see the labels every day.

Spreading the word: If your school has a daily or weekly student bulletin, ask if you can include a regular 'Word of the day' or 'Phrase of the week' feature. To save your sanity, produce a list for the term and give the list to the person producing the bulletin so that it is his or her job to include your word or phrase every day. Include a range of interesting and amusing words and phrases relevant to all school year groups. You can follow this up with a display of the same word and, perhaps, use the word as a screen saver on any departmental computers.

Sending subliminal messages: Put messages about the importance of language learning on your classroom door. Include a message about the importance of language learning in your email signature so that staff, students and parents see it every time you send a message. I use the quotation from Nelson Mandela which features at the start of this chapter.

Showcasing older students: Involve older students in helping out in younger students' lessons. They can add a touch of 'glamour' to proceedings and are good role models for the younger students, who may not know personally in other contexts students in the school who have continued on to GCSE or post-16 language study.

Organizing competitions: Organize quizzes and competitions with a modern languages theme. Advertise your competitions across the school so that students who have not opted for modern languages hear about what is going on and are eligible to enter. Check if the Association for Language Learning's 'Have Your Say' competition is operating in your area, and if so, enter some students.

Contributing to whole school events: Contribute a modern languages angle to whole school events. On International Book Day, get your students reading in your language. If there is a talent show, try to persuade a student to perform in the target language, or do so yourself! For Activities Week, plan for students to learn a different language, explore an aspect of culture or prepare an event with a languages theme.

Making the most of display: Use corridor display boards to highlight the work done in modern languages. If there are unused noticeboards in areas of the school other than your department, so much the better, as your message will be seen elsewhere. Try to make your corridor displays interactive, perhaps with a problem to solve or something to work out. Time consuming as it is, displays do need to be changed quite regularly in order to continue to attract attention: support staff should be able to help you do this.

Finally, one thing above all helps to raise the profile of modern languages as a subject within the school: that is being a successful department which has a reputation for excellence and which enables all sorts of students to make outstanding progress and obtain great results. That is what the rest of this handbook is all about.

Planning outstanding modern languages lessons 2

Long-term planning

Long-term planning is about establishing the big picture. In language teaching, having an overview of what the students will learn and how they will progress year on year is crucial. To an extent, language learning is cyclical: that is, students come back again and again to the same linguistic concepts and need to revisit them in different contexts. However, in order to make real progress, students need to develop their ability to understand and produce language of increased complexity. In other words, it is not enough simply to say that 'knowing more words' is good progress: it is the ability to put those words together in order to say what we want that amounts to real progress.

This might seem obvious, but sometimes assessment methods and examination systems can seem to go against this approach. I like to draw a parallel with maths teaching: to perform calculus or trigonometry, we still need to be able to add up, divide, multiply and subtract. But these basics are firmly embedded when we are young, enabling us to build on them. 'Mastery, not coverage' – a phrase first heard when the Key Stage 3 Modern Foreign Languages (MFL) Framework was introduced – is a good mantra to bear in mind when considering planning.

Long-term planning also needs to take into account what comes before and after the learning which takes place in your own school. With many primary schools teaching languages, it is our duty to build on students' prior learning in our work. Likewise, it is short-term thinking to focus on getting older students through their GCSE examination or equivalent at the expense of giving them the knowledge and skills they need to continue their language learning at post-16 and beyond.

A long-term plan should be a short but focused document. It clearly shows, in broad terms, what all students will have learned by the end of each school year. As far as learning is concerned, it is a good idea to identify key areas of focus for each year group in terms of:

- concepts/grammar
- skill development
- intercultural understanding
- contexts/content.

Frameworks or documents, such as overviews that come with textbooks help to outline possibilities: but each school is different. In a school where the priority is literacy across the curriculum, your emphasis in the long-term plan might be on building in lots of work to improve students' generic skills in this area. Nevertheless, your general aims will be clear from any national documentation available to help you (e.g. in England and Wales, the Modern Languages National Curriculum programme of study, GCSE and A-level examination specifications).

Members of the modern languages teaching team will find medium-term and individual lesson planning easier and more effective if they are clear on the key knowledge and skills which students should acquire in any given year.

Medium-term planning – The scheme of work

Medium-term planning is the department's scheme of work. Many long hours have been spent by language teachers on producing such an opus. The first point to make is that a beautifully typed scheme of work in a pristine folder is a waste of time if it is sitting on a shelf in your classroom or departmental office. The scheme of work needs to be a working document which everybody in the department contributes to and that is constantly referred to, reviewed and altered as you work through it.

Modern language textbooks generally come with a scheme of work: this is usually on a CD or online so that you can change it and make it your own. If your school uses a textbook as the basis of its work, you may feel frustrated that the book does not always cover what you want your students to learn. The golden rule here is that using a textbook is a matter of choice. The textbook should be a help not a hindrance: use it as a tool, not as a bible. For example, you may feel that there is too much in the textbook to get through by the end of the year; if so, as a team, work out according to your long-term plan priorities which bits you will use and which bits you will omit. Similarly, your department may feel that you need to follow the textbook so that your students can complete the tests at the end of each unit. But if this approach is leading to simple coverage rather than real understanding, the department needs to rethink its approach to assessment instead of following the book slavishly and worrying because you have not reached the end of chapter 2 by Christmas.

If you are working on producing or revamping modern languages schemes of work with your team, try to do so on a rolling programme so that everything is not being renewed at once. Rather than producing and completing a whole year at a time, try to work in termly or half-termly blocks. In advance, work on the unit(s) for that block of time and produce a draft; teach the unit that you have planned; collect feedback and ideas from all involved in teaching the unit (they can do this by writing on the unit overview); then revamp the unit retrospectively so that the new, improved version can be reused next year.

★ *Starting point*

When thinking about medium-term planning, there are two approaches. One is to think of the topic you want to cover or a set of materials you want to exploit, and plan around this. This means that you draw out relevant learning from the materials, but it may not be the appropriate learning for this point in the course. A second approach is to work with linguistic objectives from the outset: how do my students need to gradually build up their linguistic knowledge and skills so they get better over time? In this approach, content/topics come LAST. It is more a case of thinking about what you want them to learn, then fitting it round a context. For example, if I want my first French focus with my youngest students on their entry to secondary school to be sentence building using pronouns and regular verbs, I will be sure to choose a context that allows me to use a range of verbs with a range of pronouns. Starting with describing myself and my family would not necessarily deliver what I want, as I could quickly get bogged down with reflexives (*il s'appelle . . .*) and irregulars (*il a 34 ans, elle est gentille*). That is not to say that students will not come across these during my verb unit, but it will be easier for me to make my point if I choose a more appropriate context.

If you are working in a school that bases its work around a textbook, there may be no scheme of work other than the one which comes with the textbook itself. In this situation, you may find it useful to make yourself your own unit plan overviews to be sure you are clear about exactly what you are aiming for in each termly block.

★ *What should an outstanding scheme of work contain?*

For each unit of work, the scheme of work should specify:

- the name of the unit,
- the proposed time scale,
- the learning objectives (what students will learn to do and understand in the course of the unit),

- the differentiated learning outcomes (what students of different abilities will be able to do as a result of the unit),
- the content (topic, key vocabulary),
- teaching and learning ideas,
- the required resources,
- assessment details,
- the generic skills developed within the unit (e.g. literacy, personal learning and thinking skills, organizational skills, ICT skills).

The most important aspect of the unit plan is to be crystal clear on the learning objectives for the unit. If these are set out and understood by everybody teaching the unit, the planning of individual lessons becomes both easier and more effective.

Planning outstanding individual lessons

Let us get something clear: being an outstanding teacher every day of the week is a very tall order! Just because a lesson is very well planned on paper does not mean that all will go swimmingly when we hit the classroom. A lesson which works very well with one group on a Tuesday morning might well have fallen flat with the same class on a Friday afternoon. However, in our planning, getting into the habit of including elements which help students make excellent progress over time is vital.

Individual teachers are just that: we all have our own styles and approaches. Planning lessons is the job of the individual teacher, based on the medium-term plans. Having a set of lessons pre-planned for use across the department can be counterproductive: how can we know that students will be ready to move on to what is covered in the next lesson before we have taught the previous one? Nevertheless, when you are planning your individual lessons, make sure you have a broad notion of what will come next so that your lessons lead on from one another and the sequence forms a coherent whole.

★ *Learning objectives*

The success of your lesson depends on having appropriately challenging learning objectives.

In order to help your students be clear about what they are learning and how this fits into the 'big picture', try to make sure that your learning objectives are transferable to another context or topic. Students need to be able to see that when they have mastered what they are learning today, they will be able to use it again in another situation.

One of the problems with teaching languages is that sometimes, students seem to learn something in one unit of work, but do not then see how that learning is relevant within another topic or unit. Sometimes, too, they may have learned nouns or phrases within a topic area but may not have learned the vitally important high frequency language which forms the basis of the language. This can result in the sort of scenario where a 16-year-old learner knows the word for 'stick insect' but not the word for 'they'.

Research such as Barry Jones' work on the achievement of boys (Jones, B. and Jones, G. (2001)) tells us that students want to know what they are learning and why. Making learning objectives transparent to students and 'content free' is one way we can do this in the teaching of modern languages.

Of course, lessons need to have content and a context: but this should, when it makes sense, act as a setting for the learning, not lead it. For example, you might be working on a unit of work on the theme of family life, and be talking about what pets your students have. An appropriate learning objective for such a German lesson could be: 'Learning how to say what you have and don't have, using the verb *haben*.' By making the point of the lesson much more general than, for example, 'Learning to talk about pets', or even 'Learning to say what pets you have and don't have', you immediately make it clear to the students that the verb *to have* is the important part, not the names of the pets. You can also then build into your lesson and subsequent lessons the reuse of *to have* in other contexts so that students see the transferability of what they have learned. In this way, you are giving students a better chance of making linguistic progress and building up the blocks they need to succeed.

An effective lesson can have more than one objective, but things can start to get unwieldy if you try to plan for more than two or three. Your learning objectives for a given lesson may not just be based on subject-related skills and concepts: students might also be developing an aspect of their thinking skills, or ICT, or behaviour. If so, and this is one of the focuses of your lesson rather than a by-product, try to include these aspects within the objectives you share with your students.

★ *Learning outcomes*

It is usual to have common learning objectives for the whole class. Differentiation comes through the learning outcomes. When you are trying to clarify what your learning outcomes are, think in terms of what your students will be able to do and understand as a result of your lesson. This will relate back to your learning objective and what you set out to teach. Learning outcomes for different groups of students in your class can be expressed in different ways, for example:

Student groups	Language-based objectives	Grammar-based objectives	Skill-based objectives
All students, including low attainers, can . . .	Recognize and give short, simple examples	Name, recognize the grammar feature, give some examples	Name, recognize the skill, know how and when it is useful
Most students can . . .	Give more extended examples	Understand how the grammar feature works, know what it means, know when to use it	Use the skill
The highest attaining students can . . .	Give extended and more complex examples and use in different contexts.	Apply grammar feature in a new context	Apply the skill in a new context

★ *Sharing learning objectives and outcomes*

There are different ways of ensuring that your students know what the lesson is about, what they are learning and what they will be able to do as a result.

You will have one or several learning objectives for your languages lesson. Making this explicit to students at the start of the lesson is important.

Some schools have specific policies on how to share both aims and outcomes with students. In some schools, it is common practice to write learning objectives on the board or ask students to copy them into their book. What really matters, however, is that you talk the objectives through with your students so that they understand what they are learning and how this links with what they have already learned. Being able to link the learning with the real world makes it seem more relevant to the students.

To make sure that your objectives are based on key concepts and skills, and are transferable, it can help to phrase them in the following ways:

- Using 'how to', for example, 'Today you will learn how to join up sentences using some key connectives';
- Using a 'key question', for example, 'Today's key question: how do modal verbs work?'

When sharing learning outcomes for different ability groups, some teachers use techniques such as the two below:

- *Students must ... /should ... /could* .... Everybody in your class will manage what they MUST do; most will also be able to do what they SHOULD do; and the most able will be able to do what they COULD do.
- *All students will ... /most students will ... /some students will ...* This works in the same way.

Over time, work towards familiarizing your students with the target language needed to talk about language learning so that you can gradually start to use the target language to present your objectives and outcomes.

You do not want your lessons to be dry and predictable, but you do need to be sure that your students are clear about what they are learning. In an outstanding lesson, students might be involved in agreeing what the learning objectives should be. For example, you might introduce a task and ask your students to agree what it is that the class will have to learn before they can accomplish the task set. Similarly, your NVQ or post-16 class might be working quite independently on different projects: in this case, each student might have a different set of learning objectives which they are working on over time. Finally, you will always have an aim in mind, but that does not mean that other things may not crop up in the course of the lesson which take you on a slightly different pathway.

★ *A settling start*

Greeting students in the target language as they enter the room sets a really good tone for the lesson. Having a task on display which the students know they need to get started on right away means that everybody can be engaged right from the start. This is particularly useful if the students are coming in at different times from different lessons or are agitated on arrival. Make sure the task is clear and it is obvious what students have to do. You don't want to have to do any explaining.

Ideas for 'settling' tasks include:

- unjumbling words
- matching up target language and English, or synonyms/ antonyms
- putting things in order
- correcting mistakes
- deciphering codes.

Get your students into the habit of starting on the task as soon as they come in. Encourage those who are doing the task by giving them attention. Try to get students used to the idea that they do not need to finish the task, just do as much as they can. Finally, when you are ready to start the lesson, have a quick self-checking method of revealing the right answers so that students' attention does not wander.

★ *More stimulating ways to start*

Settling activities are for quietening your students down; at other times, you want a start to your lesson which wakes students up and really gets them thinking and ready to learn.

In modern languages lessons, starter activities work best if they are linked to your lesson content or recap what students learned last time. It can also be effective to have a series of 'standalone' starters which do not have a direct link to a particular lesson but are linked to each other; for example, a series of pronunciation starter activities which explore and practice different sounds, or a series of examination questions which require the same skill (such as reading gap fills).

Effective lesson starters involve everybody in your class and get students thinking. Always beginning your language lesson with whole class question and answer work, for example, can leave some students uninvolved and unengaged.

Types of activity which work well as stimulating starters include the following.

Find your partner
Students are given a piece of information on a card. They need to find the person in the class who has information which matches or complements theirs (e.g. who has a word containing the same sound; who has part of the same verb; who has a description of the same famous person). This involves moving around the class, talking to each other in the target language.

Find somebody who . . .
Students move around the class to find students who fit certain categories (e.g. who has been to France; who likes East Enders).

Getting in order

Students are in groups of four or five. Each person has a big card with a word on it. You call a sentence which can be formed with some or all of these words, and the students stand in a row with their words in the correct order. You can have a pile of words to select from if you want to expand the task.

Ask the picture

In pairs, students are given a picture and have to create three questions about it. They exchange pictures with another pair and ask their questions.

It's in the bag

Have a set of objects in a bag. Ask students to make up a scene including all the objects. You can also do this with a bag of words: draw out two words and ask students to create a sentence containing both words. You can use unusual words as long as they are cognates.

The Generation Game

Provide a set of words and ask students to generate as many correct sentences as they can from this limited set of words.

What is the question?

Provide an answer (e.g. *Gonzilla; in the shower; the day after tomorrow*) and ask students to see how many questions they can generate for that answer.

Techniques like these are useful to try to ensure that everybody is involved in the lesson right from the start:

- Use mini-whiteboards and ask students to display their answers.
- Ask students to use gestures or movement (e.g. thumbs up/down; standing up/down) to indicate their responses.
- Ask students to work in pairs. For activities which require students to think and puzzle things out, this is crucial.
- Get students moving around and talking to each other. This could be in the target language, but might also be in English, for example, if students are asked to form physical sentences.

★ *New learning*

This is the key part of the lesson. So try not to take up too much time with preliminaries and strike while your students are ready to take new things in.

There are different ways of presenting new language, for example:

- audiovisual presentation using flashcards, PowerPoint or the interactive whiteboard;
- text-based presentation using a textbook or other resources;
- audiovisual presentation using props/authentic resources;
- group or pair-work problem-solving task.

If the point of your lesson is to work on a language skill, then modelling that skill – that is, demonstrating the skill while talking through your thoughts with the class – can be a good way in.

The key when planning is to try to ensure that the students are involved in discovering and working out the new learning, rather than just being presented with it on a plate. In addition, try to intersperse any presentation part of the lesson with pair work or paired discussion so that students are not focused on listening to you for too long at any one time.

★ *Practice*

Practice is a vital aspect of language lessons. Students need the chance to hear and use the language they are focusing on so that they become familiar with how it sounds and how it works. Only after a suitable amount of guided practice can the students move on to using the language for themselves. Practice might take the form of drills, textbook exercises, games or any one of the range of activities described in the following chapters. The important thing is that students understand that they are practising and that you treat mistakes as an opportunity for learning.

★ *Application*

Sometimes modern languages lessons can stop at the practice stage. If the students are not given the chance to apply what they have learned in context and in their own way, they will not learn to become independent manipulators of the language. So having a chunk of the lesson in which students can be creative and use the language for their own purposes becomes crucial.

Tasks which allow students to apply their learning include:

- Oral presentations (e.g. weather forecast, presentation of ideal school);
- Written pieces (e.g. poem, account, diary entries);
- Oral sketches (e.g. estate agent, awkward meeting, job interview);
- Designing and making things (e.g. a board game, a grammar machine, a pronunciation guide, a phrase book);
- Preparing resources to teach others (e.g. a grammar song or chant, tongue twisters, PowerPoint presentation);
- Producing material for younger pupils (e.g. a reader, a game, a song);
- Oral interviews (e.g. TV talk show, sports person, discussion between target language and UK school pupil);
- Interacting with reading sources (e.g. website, magazine, newspaper) to accomplish a real task (e.g. choose and book a hotel according to constraints; choose outfit for a party with budget);
- Written or oral adverts (e.g. for local product/place);
- Oral dialogues around a computer animation;
- *Photostory* presentations with oral commentary;
- Oral reconstruction of a TV programme (e.g. *Big Brother, X Factor,* family scene from soap opera);
- Designing quizzes/teaching exercises (e.g. using *Who Wants to be a Millionaire* template);
- Producing a film story board;
- Producing a learning poster for the classroom (which crystallizes key learning points).

(Copyright Suffolk County Council, Making the Most of 100 Minute Lessons), 2010, p. 7.

★ *Choice*

Whenever possible, try to include an element of choice within the lesson. This helps to give the students ownership of what they are doing and makes them more likely to want to do it. During language lessons, you can allow students to choose:

- who they work with,
- which order to do tasks in,
- how they present information (e.g. as bullets, as a paragraph, as an oral sketch),
- what level of difficulty to work at.

★ *Planning for differentiation*

In your lesson planning, you will have already thought about your expectations for different groups of students when you considered your learning outcomes. As you plan each part of the lesson, think about how you will stretch and challenge the most able while supporting the least able.

Suggestions for slower learners include:

- providing extra support material (e.g. a word list with translations),
- pairing up with a more able student,
- simplifying a task (e.g. by providing possible answers to choose from),
- requiring students to present their answers in a more straight-forward format (e.g. labelling a picture).

Suggestions for the more able students include:

- providing more complex support material (e.g. two or three more advanced words),
- pairing up most able students together,
- allowing students access to resources to find more unusual words,

- requiring students to present their answers in a more challenging format (e.g. as a formal letter).

★ *Plenaries*

Throughout the lesson, give the students the chance to recap and reflect on what and how they are learning. These 'mini-plenaries' will give you the chance to see how your lesson is going and whether you need to redirect things. At the end of the lesson, use the plenary to make sure that the lesson has been effective.

Plenaries can have different purposes and are most effective when you use a variety of approaches according to need. The best plenaries will involve *all* the learners in reflecting on their learning and how they have learned. In modern languages lessons, you can use the plenary session to:

- summarize what has been learned to help students understand and remember;
- check that students understand a key concept and its importance;
- get students to think about *how* as well as *what* they have learned;
- give the class a sense of achievement so that they leave feeling they have learned something concrete;
- get students to make links to prior learning or how to apply what they have learned in other subjects;
- allow students to evaluate their own and each others' work.

Some suggestions for plenary activities:

- Ask a student to come to the board and explain the key learning (e.g. how to form the future tense) to the rest of the class. Sit in the student's seat. Encourage the rest of the class to ask questions during the explanation. Put your hand up and ask some questions yourself if appropriate.

- Ask students to work in pairs and write three sentences which use the new language. Get each pair to swap its sentences with another pair, who must check the sentences and underline the language being focused on. Ask for volunteers to read out a sentence. The whole class must stand up/stick their thumb up when they hear the structure in the sentence.

- Get students to work in pairs to come up with examples of how language learned today could be applied in the classroom situation (e.g. I haven't got a brother → I haven't got a pen; we can go into town → can we work with a partner?).

- Show students how to access for themselves grammar section/ verb tables relating to what they have been learning. Ask students to use them in pairs to find answers to a couple of questions you set.

- Display a set of sentences with mistakes. Get students to correct the mistakes and justify their response by explaining what was wrong.

- Ask students to make up an exercise to practise the new language. Students can swap and do each others' exercise in class or for homework, or you can use some of the exercises as a starter in the next lesson.

- Give students some new verbs, adjectives or other words which you have not used in class. Get them to apply the rules they have learned to these new items.

- Ask a student or pair of students to demonstrate an oral task carried out during the lesson. Tell the rest of the class to put their thumbs up when they hear something good. When this happens, ask the student or pair to freeze, and get one of the students with thumbs up to explain what they thought was good. This plenary can be used to promote the use of correct terminology, for example, intonation, conjugation.

- Ask students to spend a few minutes learning by heart the key vocabulary or language you have covered. Take feedback on which items are difficult to learn. Ask the students to suggest ways of remembering the tricky ones.

- Ask students to sort out words they have learned into nouns/verbs/adjectives. Ask them for effective ways of remembering this.
- Ask students to make up three sentences from different contexts using the words they have learned.

Language games can make effective plenaries, but you need to try to be sure that they are getting at students' understanding, rather than merely recapping what has happened in the lesson.

Homework

Like other aspects of the lesson, homework needs to be planned. Make it clear to students how homework fits in with your objectives and show them you think the homework is important by taking the time to explain and/or model it properly for them. Establish a regular timetable for when you will give homework and try to set it during the lesson rather than at the end. Ensure that students have what they need to do their homework: if your students have no access to textbooks at home, make sure they have what is required in their exercise books or have whatever resources they need.

Vary the types of homework you give. When possible, give students a choice: this makes it more likely that they will do it. Be careful you do not end up setting meaningless worksheets just for the sake of it: this can all too easily end up as a waste of time for the student and yourself as you wade your way through 30 very similar responses. In addition to the more traditional types of homework tasks, consider the following.

★ *Learning homework*

Although it might seem old-fashioned, you do need to ask students to learn vocabulary and grammar. You can ask them to learn the meaning of words, how to say and/or spell them, and how to use them in sentences. Make their learning more interesting and successful by:

- Getting students to suggest strategies they will use before they do the learning.
- Getting students to try out different strategies for learning words and report back on which are successful.
- Changing your method of testing learning so that there is variety, for example, from English to the target language; from the target language to English; hearing words and writing them down; seeing words and translating them; testing a partner on any five words; writing down any five they can remember from the words learned; correcting errors in a list of the words; using mini-whiteboards; including any five words in a sentence.
- Teaching others at home the set of words.
- Phoning or texting a friend in the evening to test each other.

★ Research homework

Check that students have internet access at home or can use the school's facilities to do their homework. Set information-gathering tasks related to the culture of the language you are studying.

★ Producing resources for use in class

This can be a motivating and useful type of homework task. For example, you can ask students to:

- prepare a set of grammar notes for their partner;
- prepare a starter (e.g. anagrams of today's vocabulary, coded sentences, an odd-one-out activity) which they can give to their partner next lesson;
- prepare practice exercises for other students to try next lesson (e.g. gap-fill tasks, sentences in the wrong order, a set of questions on a text, a set of 'Who Wants to be a Millionaire?' questions);
- produce practical resources for use in class next time, for example, a small clock with moveable hands, a set of number cards, a

set of topic-related picture cards, a pronoun dice, a verb 'ready reckoner'.

On the day the homework is due and you plan to use it in class, make sure you have an alternative duller activity for those who have not done the homework task. This will help them to feel 'left out' and hopefully encourage them to do their homework next time.

★ *Speaking preparation homework*

Students can prepare for classwork at home. Example tasks might include:

- During the register I'm going to ask you . . . so be ready with your answer.
- Prepare the longest sentence you can about . . .
- Speak for a minute without hesitation on . . .
- Prepare a 30-second presentation on . . .
- Ask questions at home to prepare your viewpoint on . . .

★ *Web-based homework*

Some schools have subscriptions to particular websites, such as Linguascope, www.linguascope.com, so that students can work on these at home. There is also a range of free websites with practical activities for students to do as homework, such as MYLO, www.hellomylo.com.

Organizing your resources

As a modern languages teacher, you have a lot of resources to manage. Keeping these organized will help to keep you sane and your lessons flowing.

While what helps the students learn best should always be at the top of your priorities list, try to avoid printing out reams of worksheets. If you can, make adjustments to worksheets before they are printed so that they can be reused, for example, number questions so that students can answer them in their books instead of on the sheet. Less able students sometimes do benefit from being able to write on the sheet, so do not hesitate to give them a worksheet if it will mean they learn better. Recycling sheets means reusing them with different classes and then filing them for next year. Keep sheets stored in a filing cabinet or drawer system so that the resources for a unit are kept together. Getting sheets printed in different colours for different units or levels of difficulty can be helpful.

When you are making up sets of cards, try to get each set made on a different colour, so that when they are being collected at the end of an activity, different sets do not get mixed up. At the end of a speaking activity, ask students to collect each set of cards together and collect them in right away. Keep an elastic band round each set and store in a plastic zipped envelope along with the resources for the unit.

Teaching students how to listen 3

The importance of listening

Being able to make sense of what you hear is a key part of learning a foreign language. We usually respond to what we hear: we answer the question, move to the correct platform or start to laugh. For students, listening to the foreign language can be challenging as it is easy to feel out of your depth quite quickly.

Listening in modern languages is a skill which needs to be taught, not just tested. It can be hard for us as teachers to know how to help our students to improve their listening skills. This is what we will look at in this chapter.

Listening as a practice activity

In the modern languages classroom, we ask students to listen in a way they perhaps rarely do in other lessons or indeed in their outside lives. They are required to really concentrate on what they hear so that they can make sense of it. I have found that students tend to think of formal listening activities as 'tests': the CD is playing, there is a grid to complete, and if you do not get it, you do not get another chance because the words have disappeared into the ether! Students often lack confidence when it comes to listening, then either start to panic or give up and switch off. Our job is to try to take the fear out of listening to the target language and make the students feel that listening is not something to be anxious about, but part and parcel of learning.

Martine Pillette, in her excellent publication *L'Oreille Fine* (2005), puts forward the idea of making many more opportunities in class for listening as a practice activity. The traditional approach to listening is almost always based on comprehension activities; Martine suggests that we as teachers make more use of our own ability to speak the language in order to get students more relaxed about hearing the language and responding to it in different ways. One way of doing this is by inventing short listening activities which become a kind of 'limbering up' activity, improving students' listening skills in a non-threatening way. They make excellent starter activities but can also be used during the lesson itself. To help engage your students in such listening practice activities:

- Use cognates as much as possible.

For example, say some random adjectives and ask students to spot which ones could be used to describe a house. Include cognates which the class has not met before.

- Ask students to give a physical response to what they hear.

For example, they can indicate if what you say is true or false, right or wrong, possible or not possible, logical or illogical, kind or unkind. They can also indicate if they agree or not, or would answer *yes* or *no* to your question.

- Try to create tasks which are open ended and do not have just one correct answer.

For example, you can ask the class 'Would you like this for Christmas?' and then list words, including plenty of previously unknown cognates.

- Exploit younger students' interest in you as their teacher.

Ask them to make judgements on things you say about your-self, for example, 'Do I prefer chocolate or sweets?' As they cannot possibly know the right answer, the activity feels more like a game.

- Include humour to help students to feel relaxed.

Activities like these are resource-free; therefore, the preparation required comes down to you thinking through what you are going to say.

Finding listening materials

Your own expertise in the target language is, of course, the prime source of listening material. Whenever you use the target language in class, your students are developing their listening skills. Do not be afraid to use your own voice in class to give students plenty of listening practice: while you may not be a native speaker, it is still very valuable for your students to be exposed to the language through your voice.

Nevertheless, it is also important for learners to hear a variety of native speakers in different contexts so that they become familiar with language spoken at near normal speed. You may be fortunate enough to have a Foreign Language Assistant (FLA) working with you in which case you have ready access to somebody who can make recordings for you as needed, or, of course, appear 'live' in your classroom! The most common source of listening materials are the CDs or web-based recordings which come with the textbook course used in class.

There are other published materials which focus on the skill of listening, often consisting of a booklet of photocopiable masters and a CD. These can make useful additions to your resource bank. The web is also an excellent source of listening materials, particularly for older students, as film extracts, video clips, TV or radio shows and songs all make excellent starting points for listening tasks.

Listening for gist and detail

Getting the gist of what you hear is an important aspect of language learning for real situations. To develop your students' skills, you can use dialogues and conversations from textbook CDs or other sources. Instead of asking students to listen purely for comprehension, or to answer the questions given in the book, you can help them to gain an overview of what they hear by finding out, for example:

- What are we listening to? (e.g. a conversation/radio programme/ set of instructions)
- What are they talking about?
- Where are they?
- How many people are talking?
- Do they sound happy or sad?
- Are they adults or children?

In this way, you can help to get students more focused on listening for gist. You can get the students to tell you how they came to their decision so they build up their skills in listening for clues in context. Do this by asking them to jot down key-words, phrases or other clues (e.g. background noises) which helped them get the gist of what they heard.

You can build up the students' skills in listening for detail by:

- Asking students to spot words in a passage of speech/video (e.g. students stand up or raise their hand when they hear a given word or word on a theme; students tick off or order words on a list as they hear them).
- Displaying a range of similar but slightly different English sentences, and asking students to indicate which one they hear. Using negatives in these sentences, for example, helps students to become more skilled at spotting these.
- Cutting up the text of a dialogue or song and asking students to order the text.

- Asking students to collect words or phrases they hear of a certain type (e.g. types of food; expressions for giving opinions; past tense verbs).
- Giving students English phrases and asking them to spot the target language equivalent.

Of course, vocabulary knowledge underpins the application of listening skills so that students are able to actually understand what is being said. Comprehension activities which can be used with sound extracts or video include:

- answering questions on what they hear,
- true/false statements,
- correcting errors in a series of statements,
- filling in the gap in a clozed text,
- choosing the right ending for sentences about the text,
- ordering images/sentences linked to the text,
- summarizing,
- matching (e.g. images, names, sentences) with what is heard,
- selecting the most appropriate caption or image for what is heard.

If students have something concrete to do during a listening activity, they are much more likely to behave properly, participate and therefore learn. You can liven up the sorts of activities above, for example:

- Get students to 'place their bets' and fill in answers *before* they have heard the text. Their 'answer' will be a complete guess: but the activity itself then becomes more fun as they listen to each item to see if they have guessed correctly.
- Use sets of cards; this requires students to physically move things in response to what they hear.
- Use mini-whiteboards as you move through an exercise, with students displaying their responses as you go.

Organizing listening activities

Modern languages textbooks come with CDs for listening practice. Some courses have an ICT-based version of their materials for classroom use which makes accessing the listening materials even easier. The teacher's book which comes with the published course contains transcripts of all the recorded material and it is vital that everyone teaching the course has a copy.

Whether or not you are using a textbook, you will definitely be giving your students practice in listening to recordings of native speakers. When you are using CDs or ICT to access recordings, you need to be prepared. Make sure you know the exact tracks you need and note them in your planner so that you can get to them right away. Use the 'time' measurer at the bottom of the screen to note down exactly where you need to start. If you are using CDs, at the start of the day or the night before, it is a good idea to look out all the ones that you need.

Some current courses have electronic versions available which include an online version of the textbook. From here, you can click directly into the listening activities: a godsend in terms of classroom organization and time saved on preparation. You can also display the transcript during correction so that students can see in print what they have just heard.

Most of the time, you will be doing listening tasks as a whole class. I like to prepare for a listening comprehension task with certain specific steps:

1. Ask the class to prepare what they need to record their answers, for example, copy the grid, write down numbers 1–9.
2. Ask the students to analyse the task and work out what they have to do. You may want to ask them to anticipate the sort of answers they are looking for.
3. Do an example and model to students how to record their answer. I like to invent an example and say it myself in a squeaky voice,

as fiddling around with the CD to play the first example can slow things down too much.

4. Check that the students understand what to do (e.g. with thumbs up/down).
5. Play the CD, one section at a time, pausing after each section if necessary. The task will run more smoothly if you play the whole exercise once and then repeat the whole thing, rather than trying to repeat each individual section.
6. Mark the task with the class.
7. Find out from the students what the common areas of difficulty are and make sure they have learned from this.

Apart, perhaps, from the analysis of the task by the students, the whole of this sequence can be done in the target language. It is important to ask students to work out what they think they have to do, as this helps to get them used to analysing the format of tasks and trying to figure out the meaning of any instructions for themselves.

Asking students to anticipate the sort of answers they might hear helps them to focus their thinking and revisit possible vocabulary areas in their heads. For example, if they need to find out *when* something happens, students need to anticipate that they might hear a date, a day of the week, a time, or a year, for example. I sometimes ask my students to think in pairs and brainstorm the sort of vocabulary they might hear for a given question so that they are more prepared when the task begins.

Correcting listening tasks by asking students for the answers can easily become tedious unless you are working with a small group. I prefer to quickly display the answers and ask students to mark their own work so that valuable class time can be used to focus instead on common areas of difficulty.

If you are fortunate enough to have a set of laptops or computers with headphones at your disposal, try to make full use of these for listening activities. You can have the whole class listening at the same time, or have groups of students listening while others do something else. The main advantage is that students can listen at their own pace. They are in control of the task and gain in confidence if they are able to listen again. I have found that students tend to respond much more positively to listening activities when they are able to access the materials for themselves. In some schools, there is a language laboratory in which students can listen to tasks at their own pace. It is worthwhile preparing an answer sheet so that students can mark their own work when they have finished. It is also a good idea to have transcripts available so that learners can self-check sections they find difficult before resorting to looking at the answer sheet.

Perhaps you feel that your students will simply look at the answers or transcript rather than listening properly to the source material. I would argue that teaching students how to be responsible for their own learning is part of what we are trying to do, so they need to learn that perseverance and self-organization are important aspects of language learning (and life!). Mathematics textbooks often have the answers at the back and students learn to be disciplined enough to use these to help them learn: we are aiming to encourage the same approach.

Listening and differentiation

If you are able to have students listening individually, you can direct them to different tasks from the materials you are using. Many websites and commercial ICT packages, including those supporting specific textbooks, have materials which are flagged up at different levels. If only a few individual laptops are available, students can take it in turns within the classroom to work on a listening task while the others do something else.

When the whole class is listening together to a task, they are, of course, all listening to the same thing. One way of catering for different abilities is to ask students to find different sorts of information. For example, everyone might be expected to listen and note down the hobby each person does. Some might also be asked to note down how often each person does his or her hobby. The most able might also be required to note down each speaker's opinion of his or her hobby as well.

Another way of differentiating is by providing different levels of support. You might provide a transcript for some students to follow as they listen to what is in the CD. You could make a set of cards with answers on to be put in order for the less able, while the more able have to note down the answers. You could provide multiple-choice answers for the less able while the more able are expected to work out the answer for themselves. Gifted students might be asked to try to write out what is being said, or note down a certain number of new words from the task, working out how they might be spelled from what they hear.

In order to stretch and challenge your students, try to give them the chance to push themselves so that they do not just opt for the 'easy option'. For example, if you do produce a 'help sheet', tell students to keep it face down on the desk and not look at it unless they really have to. Likewise, if you produce multiple-choice answers for a task, have them on a section of the sheet which can fold away. Tell the students they should keep this folded away and only look at it as a last resort.

Helping students get better at listening

It is easy to write in a student's book or report that his or her listening skills need to improve. It is much trickier to give students specific advice on what to do to improve.

When you have done a listening exercise in class with a number of marks available, you can ask students to add up their total score. Some teachers ask students to indicate what score they achieved so that they can see how the students have done. If you do this, it is a good idea to start with a low score and move up, so that everybody gets the chance to raise his or her hand and then hands are gradually lowered. You can do this in the target language, for example, *Who has scored at least 4 out of 10? At least 5?* In order to keep track of students' progress, I sometimes go round with my mark book and ask students their score for the listening activity while they are working on the next task. I record their score in my mark book so that I have a record of how well they did.

Textbooks often give an indication of the national curriculum level or potential examination grade of a listening text or task. At some points, it may be useful to tell the students that if they have managed to accomplish a particular task, it is evidence of them being able to cope with work at a given level. However, it is worth remembering that the English National Curriculum levels refer to an ability to understand and cope with passages and dialogues of a certain length and type. It does not make sense to take a given passage with questions on it and relate the amount of marks scored to different National Curriculum levels: it is more a matter of saying that if you scored above a certain amount, you are able to cope with work at this particular National Curriculum level.

None of the above actually helps students to get better at listening, however. The key question to ask yourself is: what have the students learned from completing the listening activity? This is why I prefer to follow up listening activities by asking students about common errors. This can be a discussion about which question(s) caused the most problems and why that was. Using the board, you might illustrate to your students the part of the text which was problematic, or play that extract to them again. As a result, you might ask students to note a particular vocabulary item or structure which tripped them up. You might add some other examples of this same feature so that students come away from the activity having learned something which will improve their performance next time they do such a task.

Listening for pleasure

Film and video are the ideal medium for getting students to listen to the target language in a pleasurable way.

Over the years, the BBC and Channel 4 in particular have produced a range of TV programmes specifically for school students learning languages. You can visit their websites to find out what is scheduled to be broadcast. The programmes tend to be broadcast in blocks during the night so that you can easily record them, and some are available through the TV stations' websites and on DVD. You may well find that your school has a range of recorded material already. Although some of these TV programmes were produced some years ago, there are still some gems around which your students should enjoy. Most importantly for you and your workload, the series are backed up with web-based materials such as transcripts, vocabulary sheets and activity worksheets. These resources help to focus students and ensure that they learn something concrete from watching the programmes.

Videos lend themselves to activities such as reconstructing dialogue to go with images, anticipating what will happen next and continuing the dialogue or 'dubbing' films into English, for example. With video material you can also, of course, use any of the activity types described earlier. However, do be wary of asking students to do too much so that watching the programmes becomes a chore instead of an enjoyable experience.

Thanks to the internet, there is a wealth of videos available through sites such as YouTube. These include real TV shows and film clips as well as home-produced masterpieces. When using clips from sites such as YouTube, do be sure to view the entire clip before showing it to students so that you are sure there is nothing inappropriate in the images or language used. I sometimes use an extract from a familiar quiz show as a starter: shows like *Who Wants to be a Millionaire?* and *The Price is Right* have European versions. Students find it easy to catch on to what is happening as they are familiar with the context and the shows often have visual support, such as the questions being displayed. Adverts are another good quick starter as they usually contain relatively clear language with strong visual support as well.

Authentic target language feature films and short films are an excellent and motivating way to get students listening. The British Film Council website has some helpful suggestions for films to use and ideas to exploit them. Of course, you can also use internationally popular films which are known to the students but available in target language versions, like the *Harry Potter* or *Twilight* series. Using films helps students develop not only their listening skills but also their intercultural understanding.

Getting students talking

The importance of speaking

Speaking is at the heart of language learning. Right from the start, we can help ourselves as language teachers if we agree and understand what we actually mean by teaching our students how to speak. Speaking is putting words together to say something. Writing things down and then reading them out is NOT speaking: that is writing and reading aloud. Equally, writing things down, memorizing them and then regurgitating the whole thing orally is not really 'speaking' either.

The ability to speak in the language means being able to be spontaneous. This might involve preparation, note taking, rehearsal and practice, but the end result must be the ability to take part in conversations and to communicate what you want to say.

If we take this approach to speaking, and share it with the students, our lessons right from the start will be built around an expectation that students will learn how to speak without first writing everything down. Examination specifications such as the current GCSE speaking assessment can seem to mitigate against this sort of approach and encourage students to learn by heart and then regurgitate. We do need to train our students to be able to reproduce the sort of language they have practised in class. But by teaching them from the start to put together what they actually want to say, we enable them to say what they want as well as perform well in examination orals.

From the start, make students aware of what you are looking for when they are speaking. Watching video footage of famous foreigners speaking English is a good place to start, so students understand the importance of communicating a message. Introducing students to terms like 'fluency', 'accent', 'intonation' and 'accuracy' means that they begin to understand what it means to be good at speaking.

A final point to bear in mind when planning for speaking is to look at your lesson plans over time to measure how much target language students are required to speak during the lesson. In the current GCSE examination, speaking is worth 30 per cent of the total marks: do students spend 30 per cent of classroom time speaking? Ensuring that students need to speak in the target language for a decent part of every lesson helps to highlight the importance of the skill in their own minds and also, of course, helps them to improve.

Classroom layouts for speaking

Set up your classroom to make it easier to get students speaking. If you are fortunate enough to have your own classroom or to have a classroom dedicated to modern languages, consider putting the students into groups of four or six to a table. This will make it easy for them to talk in their groups. It also means that there should be more room for them to move around and speak to different people. Another layout which works well for speaking is the horseshoe, with a second horseshoe within it. Students can easily talk to the person next to them, or the person behind/in front of them. Groups of four are easy to form as well. It is not as easy for students to move around the classroom, however.

You might well be thinking that this gives students more opportunities to chat with each other in English. You need to be clear about routines for getting students to turn and face you when you are teaching from the front. But it is not a bad thing to have the centre of attention focused away from you if you are trying to move away from an emphasis on teacher-centred work to a more student-centred approach.

Whole class speaking

When students are learning new material through a teacher-led presentation to the whole class, make sure you include enough repetition for them to feel confident about the language. Choral repetition may seem old-fashioned but it gives students the chance to get their tongues round the words in a safe situation. If you find it hard to get students to join in, suggest that you will ask those not joining in to repeat the phrase on their own.

With younger students, you can liven up whole class repetition by getting students to copy your tone as well as your words; for example, you can whisper, shout, sound sexy, say the words with a deliberately English accent, say them slowly or really fast. During repetition, draw students' attention to patterns so that they begin to make links between words. You can then ask students to anticipate how a word or phrase will be pronounced before drilling the whole class.

If you are presenting new work to the whole class, this may well involve straightforward question and answer practice. You might like to get student volunteers to come to the front to lead the session for a change. You can also try to avoid being the one who ask the questions all the time by getting one student to ask another once they have internalized the model question. To ensure everybody has spoken, ask the class to stand up. Students can then sit down when they have answered a question.

Try also to intersperse any whole class work with short bursts of oral pair work. I find that the 'Anything you can do . . .' technique works well. I might present something to the whole class using a PowerPoint, then do some choral repetition and whole class question and answer on what we are practising. After a short time, I set students up in pairs, with one as the 'teacher' (i.e. doing what I was doing with the whole class) and the other as the 'pupil'. After a minute or two, I ask the students to change roles before drawing them back together again for the next stage of the activity. This sort of technique helps to keep the students engaged, gives them a break from listening to me and ensures that they all have the chance to speak.

Pair work

When teaching and practising speaking with a normal-sized class, getting students to work in pairs is essential. Students get a chance to practise in the comfort of their own pairing. They can get their mouths round the sounds and 'have a go' without embarrassment. During whole class question and answer work, some students may not get the chance to speak, or utter just one sentence in the course of 20 minutes. Pair work gets everybody speaking, while giving you the chance to listen to individuals and give them advice on their work. Feedback from students indicates that they like working in pairs as it gives them confidence. However, they do need to understand why they are working in this way.

★ *Which pairs?*

Having a flexible approach to pair work and who works together is a good way of helping to personalize your lessons. If your students are sitting randomly or alphabetically in the classroom, they can work with the person next to them as their regular partner. They can get used to working with this person and feel comfortable working with him or her. At other times, you might like to pair students up according to ability. This is particularly useful if you have a choice of task or want to provide specific support for the least and/or most able. At times, you may choose to deliberately pair students up so that a strong student is partnered with a weaker one.

The strong student can act as a 'coach' and help the weaker student to improve.

If you quite regularly ask students to work with different people, they become used to being more flexible. I like to point out to them that in any workplace, they will need to work with all sorts of people, whether they like them or not. It is therefore good training to build up these sorts of social skills in the modern languages classroom.

★ *Changing pairs*

Pair work should not always be a sedentary activity. Giving the students the chance to move around to talk to a variety of classmates can lift a relatively mundane practice activity. When you first try this, number the students alternately as 'A's or 'B's. Then, during the activity, tell the 'A's to stay seated, while the 'B's move around the classroom, sitting in a vacant seat next to an 'A' and talking to them. When they have finished, they stand up, look for another empty seat, and talk to a different 'A'. This is quite a controlled activity and a good way of getting your students moving without too much chaos! This activity, which you can trendily call 'speed dating', is a popular one with students as they get the chance to engage with lots of their classmates.

When you feel in control of pair work done in this way, you can try a more open approach. Students have an oral task to do and must carry out that task with a given number of students in the time set. Everybody gets up and walks around the classroom, finding a partner, talking to him or her and then moving on to somebody else. In this activity, it can be useful to act as a 'matchmaker', finding 'spare' students and getting them together for the dialogue.

Maybe it seems a bit hackneyed, but carrying out surveys among their classmates is a great way to get students talking to each other and moving around. In essence, students have a set of questions to ask. They go around the class, speaking with different people, asking and answering the questions.

They record the answers on a grid. Students can give their own answers or they can answer using a cue card. At the end of such an activity, it is good to have some sort of summing up of the outcome. For example, students could produce the results as a graph or bar chart. Another approach is to award different scores to different answers given during the survey. For example, in a survey about household jobs, students could be scored according to how often they do a task (every day = 5, often = 4, sometimes = 3, rarely = 2, never = 0) and the scores could be added up to see who would make the best husband/wife/partner.

★ *Classroom management*

Establish clear conventions and routines for pair work. At the start of the year, one of my five classroom rules is 'Be a good partner'. Explain to students how much extra practice they will get at speaking if they work in pairs rather than merely speak with you one at a time during whole class question and answer work. Demonstrate to them what being a good partner means: eye contact, encouraging body language, listening to what your partner says, and giving quality feedback. This helps students stay focused in pair work as they can see a point in listening as well as speaking.

When setting up pair work, always use the same key phrase and, if possible, clear key cognate so that students know what they are about to do. To quickly get students into a role, I give them a few seconds to decide who will be Partner A and who Partner B. I then say 'Partner A?' and watch as all the 'A's raise their hand, then do the same for 'Partner B?' It is then easy to delegate roles within the pair-work task as appropriate.

Once students start to work on a task, position yourself at the side or back of the room, so that you have an overview of what everybody is doing. From this vantage point, check that everybody is getting started and knows what to do. Rather than calling to pairs from this position, walk up to students who are not on task and make sure they know what to do.

During the task, take the opportunity to listen properly to pairs of students and give them feedback on what they are doing. This is a good chance to have some individual contact with students. Focusing properly on three or four pairs of students and giving them constructive feedback is a more effective use of your time than flitting from pair to pair: the latter approach will let you check if the students are on task, but might not help them to make progress and improve.

You also need to establish a convention for stopping pair work; when 30 pupils are in full flow, this can be tricky! You need to attract their attention, and a bicycle hooter or bell can be a good way of doing this. One hoot on the hooter means stop talking or return to your place. Some teachers borrow the technique from drama of putting their hand up and waiting for students to notice, put their own hand up and stop talking.

You might tend to avoid pair work because you find it difficult to keep students on task. Perhaps they simply speak too much English or start to chat about something else completely. Like any other lesson task, pair-work tasks need to be appropriately challenging and engaging: below you will find some ideas. Secondly, if a few students are not tackling the task as they should, consider this question for the class as a whole: do students get more out of the lesson when 24 of them are speaking with each other in the target language while six are not, or when one student is speaking and the other 29 are sitting passively, perhaps listening, perhaps not?

★ *Answer gap tasks*

Answer gap tasks are tasks in which one partner has some information which the other partner needs to find out. For example, Partner A has a blank grid with the headings NAME/AGE/BIRTHDAY in the target language and Partner B knows this information. Partner A must ask questions to find out the information he or she needs from Partner B: that is the answer gap. Other examples of answer gap tasks include incomplete school timetables to fill in; pictures to describe to each other; diaries with missing information to complete; statistics to find out from each other.

Many textbooks come with resources such as cards for answer gap activities. You can often save yourself a lot of work by getting the students to produce the resources themselves. For example, there may be a set of questions which you want older students to practice:

> *What are your favourite subjects?*
> *What subjects don't you like?*
> *What job would you like to do?*
> *Why?*

Give students a piece of paper or card on which they write in English or quickly draw some answers to each question (e.g. two subjects for each question, one job and one reason). Gather these in and redistribute them randomly. Each student now has a set of answers to give and an answer gap has been created. Younger students can prepare a little clock using the lid of a round cream cheese box, two cardboard hands and a paper fastener. The answer gap comes when each student sets his or her clock at a time and they take turns to guess the time on their partner's clock.

The idea behind the game 'Battleships' provides a rich source for modern languages pair-work answer gap activities, as students need to ask questions over and over again in order to find out some hidden information. Making a repetitive practice task into a game makes it much more engaging.

Similarly, ordinary textbook speaking activities can be given a lift by making them into memory games. Often students are given a set of information to talk about. To make the task more engaging, ask all students to study the task carefully. Then ask Partner As to close their books while Partner Bs are allowed to look while they carry out the pair-work task. Rather than just putting what is in the book into the target language, Partner A has to try to remember what is in the book. This will involve the student in trying out different responses as he or she tries to find the right one, therefore getting more practice.

★ Giving pair work a focus

Practice activities can lack focus. It is a good idea to give pair-work activities a linguistic focus, depending on what the point of your lesson is. For example, if students are learning a specific tense, you can say to the class as a whole: 'While you are doing this task, I want you to look out for your partner's past tense verbs: have they got the correct auxiliary verb? Is their past participle correct?' If you are working on pronunciation, make the focus specific: 'I want you to listen to see if your partner pronounces the Spanish days of the week correctly, with a good j sound and nicely rolled rs.'

★ Coaching triads

An extension of the peer-assessment technique above is to have students work in threes. Two students carry out the task while the third's job is to act as 'coach'. The coach listens to the task and gives feedback on how well the task has been done. The trio then change roles so somebody else becomes the coach. The students understand the role of a coach from the sporting world and being part of a threesome gives them more space to evaluate more effectively what the others are saying. This can take the form of some sort of written checklist or quite simply giving each other verbal feedback at the end of the task.

Group work

Students can often work together in groups in modern languages lessons to accomplish a task. In this section, however, we are looking specifically at group tasks in which the purpose of the group work is for students to speak with each other in the target language.

★ *Group discussions*

Greg Horton from the Wildern School in Hampshire has done some innovative work on getting students talking in groups (European Award for Languages, July 2008). His approach is based upon the fact that students like giving their opinions about things which matter to them. Students are systematically taught phrases for expressing opinions, agreeing and disagreeing. In groups, they are given some sort of visual stimulus. This might be a catalogue page of some clothing, some postcards of possible holiday destinations, or even just a set of school subject cards. In their groups, students have a discussion about what they see, expressing their opinions and arguing with each other. Their discussion can be supported by a laminated sheet of the key discussion phrases, but students gradually become less reliant on this support material and more independent.

This approach really builds students' confidence and their ability to talk spontaneously, as they are required to think on their feet and say what comes into their head. The talk is carefully scaffolded, but neither scripted nor learned. Most importantly, students respond really well to being able to give their opinions, especially boys.

★ *Board games*

Playing a board game is a great way of getting students to speak to each other and practise language. You have two layers: the language they need to actually play the game, and the language to talk about playing (i.e. 'It's your turn' etc.). For example, a good game to practise describing people is the game 'Guess Who'. But very effective language learning games can be produced by students themselves for other students. Give a group of students a set of criteria for producing a language learning game and they will be very creative. The key is that students need to speak to each other to play the game. Challenges and forfeits can be built into the game so that students use the language they are focusing on.

★ *Drama-based activities*

Most students enjoy acting things out and this is another fruit-ful area into which we can tap as language teachers. Drama-based activities can be creative: in addition to practising the language, they can involve the students applying what they have learned in a new context, to produce something new. Examination role plays are not really drama activities: they are just a task type for getting students to use language in a given situation. Producing sketches or playlets on a theme gives students the chance to use their language while being creative.

TV programmes can provide good contexts for drama work. 'Through the Keyhole' involves describing homes; confessing things to 'Big Brother' means using the past tense to describe what *has* happened and giving your opinions about this; 'Who do You Think You Are?' could entail describing your family tree.

Another technique to use is living tableaux. As a group, students work to prepare a description or narrative of an event, for example, a past holiday. One student narrates while the others create still pictures or 'tableaux' to illustrate the narrative.

Puppets are a good way of getting reluctant learners to talk. Even post-16 learners respond to having an imaginary char-acter say what they want them to say! Creating and perform-ing dialogues between puppets enlivens any conversation.

All of these activities need to be underpinned with success criteria, so that students know what you are looking for in their work.

★ *Dilemmas*

In a dilemma-based activity, students are given a set of circum-stances and a dilemma to resolve. The dilemma is a genuine one which has no 'right' answer: in groups, students discuss, agree or disagree, and come to a solution as to what the best course of action is. This sort of activity is not a performance:

the discussion which takes place is the point of the activity as students use the language they have learned to grapple with a testing scenario. The students can be themselves for the dilemma, or can be in role. For example, colleagues in Suffolk schools have built a dilemma-based activity around the question 'Should we go on strike?' Students discuss their response to a proposed change to the school uniform in their school. In a further French example, students take on roles as members of a family from Sénégal in order to decide if the family should move to join the father, who is already working in Paris. Dilemmas are challenging activities because students are dealing with subject matter which is cognitively challenging while using their language skills.

Using new technologies to enhance speaking

Digital technology makes it much easier to record and quickly replay examples of students' spoken work. When you play this to the class, you can ask students to comment on its qualities and give some suggestions for improvement. A small handheld digital recorder for your own use is a very handy addition to your armoury of resources. Video recordings of students can also be easily made and replayed using flip video recorders, which quickly plug in to the USB port of your computer. Of course, students can make use of their own mobile phones to record their speaking work and email it to you for marking: a great leap forward on the days of having to gather in and replay bags of cassette tapes! This makes it easier for you to set speaking work as homework as well.

Students can prepare oral presentations or talks using PowerPoint. By giving them some constraints – for example, a maximum number of three word bullet points per page – you can help students to practise speaking from memory using only pictures and a few words as prompts. Similarly, students can use programmes such as Photostory to put together a sequence of photos with a voice-over. This could range in difficulty from students using their own photos to create a presentation called 'My home' to post-16 students preparing a detailed analysis of environmental issues in the target language country using photos from the internet.

Using technology to stimulate talk is an area of constant change and growth. The ability to create characters which move and talk can be exploited as students put words into the mouths of the characters they create, using Voki for example. Such programmes enable less confident learners to talk in the target language without putting themselves on the line. Who knows what the future will bring in this area? See Chapter 10 on how to ensure you keep up with new developments.

Encouraging independence

In any aspect of speaking, the students' ability to speak more independently can be improved if you use some of the techniques below.

★ Pictures and symbols

Whenever you can, use pictures and symbols instead of words when designing speaking activities. The visual clues help students know what to say but do not tell them how to say it.

★ Withdrawal of support

If you provide written support for an activity, for example, a dialogue, try to make sure you withdraw that support at some point. For example, once students have had the chance to practise a dialogue a few times, simply remove the PowerPoint slide or ask students to close their books and carry on. Alternatively, take away the ending or beginnings of sentences on the support slide, or leave the first letter of each word on display so students have a memory jogger, but not the answer.

★ *Bullets and notes*

Teaching students how to reduce down what they want to say into a couple of key words or bullets is a good skill and one which they need to practice. Once students have prepared for an activity, you can give them constraints such as '3 bullet points of 3 words', and see if they can speak from that.

★ *Spider diagrams or mind maps*

I use spider diagrams to get students to think about everything they can say in answer to a given question or on a particular topic. They can record this in the target language or in English, but must use single words or sentence starters only. They can use the spider as a prompt or structure to help them remember the kinds of things they can say.

Speaking and differentiation

Grouping students in ability pairs or groups for speaking work helps you target different pairs with different tasks. Use different coloured cards or worksheets to present your tasks so that it is easy for students to select the level they want to work at. More difficult tasks will require students to say more and use more complicated language.

Of course, you haven't always got the time to make your own resources and textbooks contain plenty of practice speaking activities. Even if you set everybody the same core speaking task, you can still differentiate to allow for different outcomes from different groups of students. You can do this by explaining what you are looking for or by jotting down on the board what you are expecting, perhaps using * and ** to show levels of difficulty. For example, the core (*) task from the book might be saying what sort of TV programmes you like and dislike; for the extended (**) version, you might ask students to include how often they watch that sort of programme as well.

To provide support for the least able during speaking tasks, you can:

- Provide word cards or the written form on a Post It© for students who find it hard to remember.
- Jot down (approximate!) phonetic transcriptions for students who keep mispronouncing key words (e.g. *2M* for *tu aimes . . .?* in French).
- Let the less able use their book for support while others speak from memory.
- Ensure the less able take on the easier role in conversations (e.g. answering rather than asking questions).

To challenge the more able, you can:

- Suggest they include extras and expand the basic task (e.g. comments on the weather, chitchat on what they did yesterday).
- Add constraints to get them thinking, such as only using sentences containing a certain number of words.
- Give them a card of more advanced phrases which they must include.
- Give them the freedom to create responses rather than be guided by cue cards or prompts.

Teaching pronunciation

In the past, language teachers in the United Kingdom sometimes OR language teaching sometimes tended to concentrate on the pronunciation of individual words rather than on patterns. As a result, students tended to rely on teachers to tell them how to pronounce every new word. Such an approach mitigated against the creation of independent and confident language learners. Teaching pronunciation properly means teaching students:

- the sounds of the language and how to make them
- how to pronounce individual letters, combinations of letters (sometimes called 'letter strings') and accents
- rules and anomalies
- intonation, tonal and stress patterns.

The amount of focus placed on these aspects depends on the language you are teaching; for example, while German pronunciation rules are fairly regular, Chinese pronunciation and tones will require a different emphasis.

Learning pronunciation rules can be enjoyable for students. It is something which all students, including the least able, should be taught so that they can feel more confident about speaking.

★ *Techniques for teaching pronunciation*

Pronunciation patterns can be taught as and when they occur in the course of lessons. Some textbooks pick out sounds within units and do explicit practice on these. You can also do this for yourself by isolating particular sounds to focus on. Over time, you need to ensure that the range of main sounds is covered so that your students have a firm grasp. As you meet these sounds again in new words, get your students to try to pronounce them before you give the correct pronunciation so that they begin to apply their skills in context. I like to display key sounds on big sheets of paper on the wall, to which we add new words containing that sound as they arise.

Some secondary schools choose to begin their Year 7 (ages 11–12 years) secondary school curriculum with a unit focusing on pronunciation. This means that students have a chance to build on their pronunciation knowledge from primary school or to acquire this if they have not previously studied the language. Rachel Hawkes from Comberton Village College in Cambridge (http://rachelhawkes.typepad.com/) and others have produced materials to support the teaching of phonics in modern languages. The pronunciation of single letters and letter strings is taught through linking a letter or letter string with a sound, an image, and a gesture. The image and gesture relate to a word containing the key sound. Students repeat and practice the word containing the sound and make the gesture at the same time. Because of the different senses involved, the technique helps learners to remember the pronunciation. The gesture becomes a shorthand way of reminding students how a letter or letter string is pronounced when they meet it in subsequent lessons.

Post-16 learners may well also be in need of a revision course in the basics of pronunciation. I would advocate again a real blitz on pronunciation at the start of the course so that patterns are clear to them and they are able to pronounce any new word correctly.

The first step towards improving students' intonation and stress patterns is to be sure you are clear yourself about which ones you will teach explicitly for your language. Do not be afraid to simplify patterns a little if it helps your students to sound a little more Spanish or Japanese when they speak.

So, for example, I teach my students to use a rising tone in their voice when they ask a question in French. You can ask students to 'conduct' each other in pairs so that they improve. Using unknown language, you can give random questions and answers and ask your students to identify which are the questions, merely from your tone. Similarly, I have improved the French accent of less able students by telling them to stress the final syllable of each word they say. To help, I get them to use a downward fist hammering-type gesture whenever they come to the last part of the word. By saying mai*son* instead of their heavily anglicized *maiso*n, their accent is immediately improved.

Help students to improve their pronunciation by highlight-ing specific aspects during whole class work and speaking exercises. During choral repetition, you can exaggerate sounds so that students pick them up. Tongue twisters, traditional or invented, make a good lesson starter. Odd-one-out activities in which students need to listen and pick out the different sound or word can help students to develop a good ear for the right pronunciation. There are more suggestions for developing students' pronunciation in the section on reading aloud in Chapter 5.

Turning students into readers 5

Being a capable reader in a foreign language is an important skill for students to develop. Now more than ever before, we are surrounded by a barrage of reading material on the web and a great deal of social communication is done through reading, for example via interacting on social networking sites and text messaging. Being able to understand text is an important element of students' overall capability in languages: not just so that they can glean factual information but also to enable them to develop and sustain friendships and interact with others.

Languages as a cultural entity are brought to life for students when they engage with authentic texts in the target language and see the language being used for a real purpose. Sometimes students equate 'reading' with 'working from the textbook' because this is the only sort of reading they do. Hence, they get quite proficient in matching names with hobbies or answering questions on a chunk of writing, but miss out on reading material which actually engages their interest or provokes real feelings or emotions, even at a basic level. Yet, if we can capitalize on the feeling of fulfilment students can have when they make sense of texts, we can help them to develop their skills sufficiently to enable them to engage with written texts both now and later in life. My husband flunked his A-level French, but his passion for jazz means that he will purchase and somehow make sense of an entire issue of the French magazine *Jazzman* whenever we go to France!

Finally, it is through reading that we improve our vocabulary and begin to internalize sentence structure and syntax. Students need to build up their proficiency in reading in order to be able to tackle longer texts without fear, make sense of them and reuse what they have met in other scenarios.

Getting some students to read anything at all is not easy, never mind getting them to read in a foreign language! It is true that reading can sometimes be neglected in schools, particularly reading authentic texts. In this chapter, we will look at some strategies and approaches to increase students' capacity to read and enjoyment in reading.

Progression in reading

For reading, progression through the National Curriculum, the Languages Ladder and examination board specifications is based on the complexity of the reading material that students are expected to understand. They move from understanding single words to short phrases, sentences, then paragraphs and longer texts. The language itself gets more complex and they become better at dealing with imaginative texts and understanding people's points of view, attitudes and emotions.

This does not mean that younger students should not be expected to interact with longer texts. Right from the start, building in longer texts to your lessons challenges students and helps them to develop the skills and confidence they need to deal with blocks of writing without being frightened. When teaching reading, it is what you do with a text rather than the text itself which is important. The same news item from the internet can be used with beginners and A-level students, provided, of course, that you do not give both groups the same task.

Another aspect of progression in reading is becoming more proficient at working out the meaning of unfamiliar language. Students progress from using textbook glossaries to being able to use dictionaries and a range of other resources. At the same time, they get better at using their brains to puzzle out meaning, through contextual clues and their own grammatical knowledge.

Really good readers enjoy reading for pleasure and use what they have learned from their reading in their own written and spoken work. They choose their own reading material and respond to it in a range of ways.

There is also a strand of reading which is sometimes overlooked: students' ability to read aloud. Even beginners are expected to quickly 'match sound to print' (English National Curriculum Attainment Target (AT) 3 Level 2); as they progress with their language learning, we should expect students to get more and more confident at reading aloud.

One final point: reading skills improve gradually and need to be built upon in a logical way. It does not make sense to reduce your lessons down to word-level work every time you start a new topic. Students who can cope with texts at the end of one unit can also do so at the beginning of the next, even if some new language is introduced.

Developing reading skills

★ *Organizing the teaching of reading skills*

The development of particular reading skills needs to be included in the scheme of work, so that students make progress in what they are able to do when faced with the written word. If literacy is a priority in your school, work with the English department to see what students learn in that subject and try to link work in modern languages with this when you can.

When planning across your team or for your individual lessons, bear in mind the different aspects of reading which you are trying to develop, for example, how to make sense of a longer text; how to read aloud properly; how to work out meaning from context; how to use reference materials successfully. For each year group, work out exactly what it is that students need to learn (and practise) in order to become more proficient, and include these in your scheme of work. Make progress in reading explicit to students by basing some lessons around learning objectives related to the development of reading skills: if you include the phrase 'how to' in your objective, it will help you to ensure that your reading objective is clear and transferable. Some textbooks include tips and strategies for the development of reading which can be worked on and developed in lessons.

★ Reading aloud

Learning how to read aloud is an important part of becoming an independent language learner and should be one of the first skills students acquire. Reading aloud is sometimes not given much attention. Yet, students need to be able to read out what they see written down if they are to make independent progress: how can you reuse a word you have found in a text or in the dictionary if you do not know how to pronounce it? How can you ask for a place name or historic monument abroad if the way you read it is unrecognizable to a native of the town you are in?

There are two aspects to reading aloud: pronouncing individual words correctly and putting the right feeling or emphasis into what you are reading. In Chapter 4, we looked at how to teach letter strings and how they are pronounced. Further activity types which help students develop their ability to match sound with print include:

- Using flashcards with letter strings or graphemes on them to practise matching sounds to letters.
- Finding rhyming words within a set of words.
- Completing rhyming couplets by selecting from a set of possibilities.
- Grouping together words which sound the same when read aloud.
- Using a model word containing a key sound to try to read (and write down) other (new) words they hear.
- Target language or English? Show and then read out a list of cognates, reading each one either in English or in the target language.

Systematically identify and work on areas which cause most problems. Some students will find it useful to record approximate phonetic transcriptions: encourage them to do this for individual sounds rather than whole words, so that they get used to the concept of building up words bit by bit, using what they know.

As well as being able to read individual words, students need to become proficient in putting the right sort of emphasis on words as they read. Teach and model intonation patterns (e.g. for French, making the tone of your voice go up for a comma and down for a full stop) and then get students to practise the same thing in pairs. You can 'conduct' the students so they get to know the intonation patterns, then ask them to conduct each other in pairs or groups as they read aloud.

Finally, students need to get better at putting feeling into what they read so that reading does not just sound stilted and wooden. You can practise this by displaying sentences or phrases on the board and asking students to read them out in different styles; for example, the target language phrase 'Are you coming to the party?' could have different meanings depending on the tone in which it is read. Another idea is to give out 'mood cards' if you are getting students to read a text aloud. Each student has to read his or her part according to the manner of the word on his or her card (e.g. *happy, enthusiastic, disappointed*) and the others guess his or her mood. Discussing this sort of thing with students and letting them experiment with different tones helps them to begin to understand the importance of aspects other than the actual printed words.

Asking students to read aloud in front of the whole class can be very off-putting for them and can lead to a loss of pace and momentum if the student is struggling. On the other hand, students need to build up their confidence and feel that they can read aloud whatever comes their way. While you are reading aloud, encourage students to follow the text with their finger or a ruler. Keep the class focused and engaged by stopping every now and then to ask a random student to read the next word. If you do get a student to read aloud in front of the whole class, help him or her out over tricky words and try not to labour over mistakes too much. I have found it much more effective to start things off by reading myself, then ask the students to continue by reading aloud to each other in small groups. Eavesdropping in on the different readers to provide support and corrections can be done much more subtly in this way.

★ *Using context and clues to work out meaning*

When you are looking at a text in class, one approach is to start by asking students to try to work out the kind of text they think it is, for example, a letter, a website article, a story, or an email message. Ask them to justify their answer so that they engage with features of the text such as layout, design and image as well as the language. In this way, students begin to learn to use context and clues to help them access texts.

You can then go on to ask your students what they think the text might be about. Ask them to look for words and other clues that help them reach their answer. Engaging with texts using a grid on which students record their thoughts and findings is a good way to get them to reflect on how they read and build up their skills. First, you could get them to look at the text for cognates or near-cognates, that is, words which are the same as or very similar to the English equivalent. You can ask them to highlight or underline these words in one colour. Next, ask them to highlight words which they know. Go on to ask students to identify words they think they can guess from the context, so that they learn how to gradually whittle away at a text to get at its meaning.

You can help students to improve their ability to work out meaning from the words around a word by giving them practice activities. Give them sentences which include unknown words and get them to try to guess what the unknown word might mean. Reward logical thinking as well as the correct answer. For example, you could use a target language sentence such as *My dog lives in a* kennel. *Kennel* is the unknown word: what might it mean? Students often tend to reach for the dictionary as their first course of action; exposing them to exercises such as this helps them to realize that the brain should be the first port of call.

When you are making up tasks such as these, make sure that you use cognates or easy language around the unknown word so that students think about the unknown word rather than struggling with the meaning of the rest of the sentence.

★ *Reading for meaning*

There are different ways to get students to work with a text to get at its meaning. The most traditional include:

- questions on the text in English or the target language;
- true/false sentences about the text: This can be made more challenging by the inclusion of a third option, 'not in text;'
- pictures to match up with the text or to put in order as they occur in the text;
- incorrect sentences in the target language about the text which need to be corrected;
- headings or headlines to be selected and/or matched with parts of text;
- summarizing the text in English or the target language;
- translation.

Even for older and post-16 students, basic activities such as these can be livened up if you set up the task within your lesson in a more active way, for example:

- Cut up the text into sections and post them around the room so that the students have to move around to find the information they need.
- Set the task as a 'collective memory' activity. One copy of the text is at the front of the class. Students work in groups to answers the questions/translate the text or whatever your task is, but only

one student at a time from each group is allowed to come up to view the text for a limited period.

- Mini-whiteboards are used for students to display their answers.

DARTS (Directed Activities Related to Text) are strategies developed in the 1970s and 1980s by Lunzer and Gardner. They encourage students to engage with texts and think about what they read, and are especially useful for involving older students in reading tasks. DARTS which work well for foreign language work include:

- *Text completion (clozed) texts*: students predict deleted words, phrases or sentences.
- *Prediction*: students predict the next part of the text.
- *Table or diagram production or completion*: students complete a table or diagram using the text, or produce their own diagram to represent the text's content (e.g. a flow chart).
- *Underlining or highlighting*: students select particular parts of the text, for example, those which back up a particular opinion.

For a more creative approach to reading for meaning, some typical 'thinking skills' activities lend themselves very well to encouraging students to read for understanding. These include the following:

Sorting activities
Pieces of text are given on card. Working in groups, students sort the cards according to a set of criteria. For example, they order pieces of text into a coherent whole; they classify statements in order of importance; they select which statements apply to the United Kingdom and which to the target language country.

Mysteries
Short pieces of information about a key question (e.g. *Will Klara marry Josef?*) are given, in the target language, on small pieces of card. The information includes some 'red herrings' and there is not one correct answer to the question.

In groups, students sift through the information, grouping the cards as they see fit, and work out what they think is the answer. They then give and justify the conclusion they have reached.

Living graphs or fortune lines

Students have a text and an empty graph shape. The axes of the graph may show, for example, happiness and time of day; or successfulness and months of the year. Students read the text and use the graph shape to plot the fortunes of the character/aspect dealt with in the text.

If you are not sure how these activities work in practice, try asking your colleagues in the Humanities department as they are very familiar with these sorts of techniques. They are especially valuable as they get students talking and discussing meaning, developing their language skills and thinking skills simultaneously. Several modern languages websites, including the Sunderland MFL website, have readymade activities for you to try.

★ Reading and differentiation

Reading is an area in which differentiation by task can be fairly straightforward. Many textbooks have texts at different levels within the same chapter: rather than everybody working their way through the whole unit, give the students a choice of task. I like to simply write on the board what the different tasks are, labelling them to show the level of challenge (e.g. * and ** tasks, or with a National Curriculum level). If you are using worksheets, you can have them printed on different colours to indicate the level of challenge. I have found that students are quite happy to choose the level they feel is appropriate for them, and students who underestimate themselves can always be directed by you towards the wiser choice.

If you are producing your own texts, word processing helps you differentiate texts with some ease. You can write a basic text, then reproduce it with some of the words in bold to help the less able. You can add in some extra bits to the same text to stretch your high attainers, so that, for example, they need to use resources to access it fully.

Finally, you can use the same text but ask students to do more challenging things with it. For example, you could use an extract from a TV listings magazine and ask students to:

- identify what it is they are looking at and explain how they know;
- find a given number of words which are the same as English words;
- find TV programmes on a certain day at a given time;
- find all the films/sports programmes/American programmes;
- find something they would like to watch and explain why;
- find something suitable for, for example, their granny to watch after 8 p.m.;
- choose a TV programme and summarize what it is about;
- give their opinion about a given programme;
- translate part of the listings into English;
- devise a conversation around what they read;
- highlight some words or phrases and reuse them in a description of a British TV programme to add to the listing.

Differentiation is also about enabling students to respond to texts in different ways: using texts as a springboard for speaking or writing is an important part of developing reading.

Reading for pleasure

★ *Finding suitable texts*

The internet is a fantastic source for non-fiction texts in the target language. Use a target language search engine (e.g. google.fr or google.de) to search for texts on a theme or news item.

It can be quite difficult to find appropriate reading material for independent reading. Some publishers produce sets of readers at different levels for secondary school students, although these are not so easy to find now as they were in the past. Cartoon books can work well as they have a good amount of visual support to aid comprehension. For whole class reading and related activities, try dipping into translations of familiar and popular texts such as *Harry Potter* or the *Twilight* series. Some classic young people's books from the target language country will also be suitable. Poetry can be accessible in that it often comes in bite-sized chunks. When abroad, I like to buy school textbooks which contain texts studied by students in the country itself, as these are always at an appropriate cognitive level. It is often possible to find a poem or text which is appropriate both linguistically and cognitively for study in class.

Teenage magazines or hobby-based magazines can entice students although the content of teenage magazine needs to be checked. Some publishers (e.g. Mary Glasgow, Authentik) produce magazines specifically directed at language learners of different abilities and these can be used very successfully to improve students' skills. If appropriate, you can ask your students to take out their own subscription so that they can get the most out of having their own magazine.

Many texts can be purchased easily and cheaply in supermarkets when you are visiting the target language country. They can also be purchased through online bookstores, including those based in the country itself, such as *Amazon.de* or *Amazon.fr*. Your local bookshop may be able to order texts for you or you can use London-based bookstores such as *The European Bookshop* or *Grant and Cutler*.

★ Organizing reading for pleasure

In an ideal world, some class time would be set aside for reading each week. In this time, students are able to choose what they would like to read. Twenty minutes devoted to this activity will help students to feel more confident about choosing and reading texts. Encourage students to engage with the text by having a reading diary in which they give their opinion of what they have read. This might be as simple as ticking a smiley, straight or sour face, or require them to write several sentences. Being able to write a book review can be a learning objective which is worked towards for several lessons so that, over time, students have the skills and language they need to record their views in the target language.

If your school has time set aside each week for reading, during registration or tutor time for example, encourage your students to read a foreign language book or magazine in that time. Many school libraries are not particularly well geared towards languages: visit your library to have a look at what is available and make suggestions. Your librarian will probably be very glad to hear your ideas.

Developing dictionary skills

Teaching students how to use the dictionary when reading is probably the easiest way into using a bilingual dictionary, as looking up words in the target language to find the English is more straightforward than the other way round. There are some published resources which focus on the development of dictionary skills and include specific activities for practising how to use the dictionary.

Key concepts which students need to understand include:

- *The dictionary is only a tool*: the brain should be first point of call.
- *The bilingual dictionary is in two parts (target language-English and English-target language)*: when reading, they will need the target language-English section.
- The heading words on each page and typeface/use of colour help you find your way around.
- *The abbreviations used can help you find the right meaning*: older students need to know the full range of abbreviations, while younger students need to know key ones only.

- The phonetic transcription tells you how to pronounce a word using the International Phonetic Alphabet but can be ignored by all but the most advanced learners.
- Sometimes a word has more than one meaning, so reading through a definition is essential.
- Not all words in a text can be easily found in the dictionary, especially verbs.

Students need to learn to prioritize when they will use the dictionary and not revert to it at the first opportunity. A good activity is to ask them to design a flow chart to show how to use the dictionary to look up a word. The first stage of the chart would be *Do I actually need to look up this word?*

Dictionary skills are one area where games and competitions can work really well. You can divide the class up into teams or get students to play in teams of two. If students use mini-whiteboards, you can monitor who understands the various processes being practised, and who does not. You can keep the score as you ask students to be the quickest to, for example:

- Find the meaning of a word you give them in the target language.
- Find the gender of a word you give them in the target language.
- Find words within given constraints (e.g. an -*er* verb beginning with *z*/ a masculine noun beginning with *t;*).
- Find the target language word for a word you give them in a sentence (e.g. I don't feel very *well*; I've dropped my keys down the *well*).
- Find three different meanings for a given target language word.
- Decide whether they could look a word up in the dictionary while you give them a range of words (including declined verbs).

In terms of languages for life, being able to make effective use of online dictionaries is crucial: if you are working on the computer as you read, it is obvious that the easiest and most practical thing to do is to use online tools. Likewise, if you are preparing students for a vocational qualification, it would make little sense to prevent them from using the tools at their disposal. Online dictionaries and translators are useful for looking up words and short phrases and for checking meaning: their use when students are writing is another matter (see Chapter 6).

Modelling how to use dictionaries and other resources successfully is a key technique. Do not be afraid to show students how you revert to a dictionary when you need to check meaning or spellings, for example. Have dictionaries readily accessible to students but actively encourage them to think 'Brain before Dictionary'.

More able students and post-16 students can be encouraged to use monolingual dictionaries when accessing text. This will help them develop their reading skills as well as build up their language as they meet synonyms and alternative ways of expressing ideas.

Teaching writing 6

Writing effectively in a foreign language means being able to put words together that get across what you want to say. Teaching students to be able to do this involves lots of steps and lots of practice.

Students need to understand what it is that makes good writing in the target language. They need to be clear that communication is key: the more information they give, the more descriptive their writing, and the more opinions they include, the better their piece will be. As students make progress, they will move from being able to write single words and short phrases to longer sentences and paragraphs. Along with the content, students need to be aware of the importance of the quality of their language. They need to appreciate that what they write is a showcase for what they know: variety of structure and range of language will be crucial aspects of a good written piece, even for younger students. Finally, students' accuracy needs to improve over time so that they can confidently put together and reproduce sentences without too many mistakes.

Planning for writing

As with the other three language skills, it is not enough to simply assume that students will learn how to write well simply through being asked to write. If you have a clear view of how to help your students make progress, and plan this into your everyday lessons, your students will begin to improve and develop their writing skills. Sometimes, the proper development of writing skills can be overlooked: a written task is left to the end of the lesson, and then has to be rushed, or is set as homework rather than worked on in class. Integrating writing as part and parcel of what students do every day is key to them seeing writing as linked to the other language skills and not as a nasty (and difficult!) added extra.

When you are introducing new vocabulary or language, do not shy away from introducing the written form. Ensure first of all that the students are familiar with and confident with how the language sounds: this will probably entail getting them to recognize and repeat. When you look at the written form, talk about spelling, making overt links to what the students know about letter strings and the sound–spelling link. Get your students to think about potential pitfalls in spelling the new language. When it is appropriate, do not be afraid to compare and contrast how the target language word is spelled compared with English.

Regularly include short writing activities as part of your lessons. Mini-whiteboards are a fabulous resource for integrating writing and building students' confidence: if they make a mistake, they simply wipe it away. I use mini-whiteboards with students of all ages: even at post-16, they are an extremely useful tool. If you do not have access to a set of mini-whiteboards, consider laminating a set of white cards. You will also need a set of non-permanent marker pens and something which students can use to wipe off their boards: I bring in a toilet roll and dole out a piece to each student! Any of the activities below can be done using pen and paper. However, the advantages of using mini-whiteboards are that students find writing more enjoyable as it becomes more like a game, with students vying to be the first to raise their board; and you as the teacher can quickly monitor students' writing. You can work together with the whole class, revealing or giving the stimulus one at a time. Lower attaining students who do not like being put on the spot will feel more confident if you allow them to work in pairs.

These ideas for quick starters or class writing activities/ games focus on writing at word or sentence level:

- unjumbling words;
- deciphering codes to find words;
- writing a verb/noun/adjective beginning with . . . (e.g. N)
- unjumbling sentences;
- correcting the mistake in sentences;
- making sentences positive/negative;
- completing sentences with any word that fits (i.e. makes sense and is grammatically correct, e.g. I've _ my cat!);
- writing a sentence that includes a given word (e.g. at, were, cockroach). You can pull the words out of a bag to make it more fun;
- writing a question for a given answer (e.g. me!, in the kitchen);
- producing as many different sentences as possible starting with a given phrase (e.g. I would like . . ., After having . . .);
- producing as many different sentences as possible from a given group of words;
- adding a word to a sentence: in groups, passing round the mini-whiteboards, adding a word at a time to what the person before you has written, trying not to finish the sentence;
- writing a sentence for your partner. He or she then decides if it is true or false/sense or nonsense.

Developing different kinds of writing

★ *Copying*

Copying accurately is the most basic form of writing. It is crucial that students are accurate copiers because if a word is copied wrongly from the board or dictionary, it is likely to be wrong for ever more! Try to avoid asking students to copy from the board when you can: constantly looking up and then down again at the paper makes it difficult for students to be accurate, particularly if they have no patterns to go by other than English ones. If students need to copy vocabulary into their books, try to get them to do this from a worksheet or textbook at their side. Practise with the students how to break the words up into syllables and copy each bit at a time. When students are beginning to learn the language, get them to write the words they are learning in the air with their finger and practice writing words on a mini-whiteboard.

Accents can be practised with different body positions to represent each one so that students know the names and shapes of different accents right from the start. Writing accented letters on a mini-whiteboard will help students get accents *on* the letters rather than beside them, as this can be quite an alien concept for English-speaking students.

Teaching students to write using non-Roman scripts brings with it its own challenges, as they have to get used to forming characters with which they may well have no familiarity. For such languages, learning to write will involve a good deal of practising the basic characters through copying, perhaps using squared paper or grids for support. As with accents, drawing characters in the air and forming them with their bodies can play an important role in embedding shapes and patterns in students' minds.

★ Writing from memory

From an early stage, teaching letter strings and what they sound like will help students to be able to write from memory. When you learn new words together, students can have a stab at writing how they think they might be spelled, again using mini-whiteboards. You can then talk about the different attempts at spelling and why they could or could not work before revealing the correct spelling. In this way, students begin to internalize patterns and make links between sound and spelling. The same process needs to happen with accents: as well as teaching students the names of the accents, teach them the sound each accent makes when it appears on or under a letter.

When you meet a set of new words, give students time in class to have a go at memorizing spellings. Then do some work with mini-whiteboards, getting students to try to write them down. Use this as a training exercise as opposed to a test: it does not matter if the students get the right answer; it does matter that they are looking at the words, spotting where they personally have difficulties, and trying to think of strategies to help them remember tricky spellings.

In the current GCSE examination, students are required to write an extended piece from memory. They know what they will be writing about and have time to prepare this in class before reproducing it in examination conditions, with a dictionary for help (or hindrance?) One response to this is to get students to memorize chunks of language lower down in the school so that they build up their techniques for memorizing essays. I would argue that this is counterproductive: we need to build up the students' capacity as writers so that they can go on to produce writing for themselves that is not a simple regurgitation of what they have prepared. Choosing carefully what students need to be able to reproduce from memory (e.g. grammatical patterns, key structures, spelling of individual words) and working with them on how to do this will stand them in better stead for writing from memory in the future.

★ *Substitution*

Substitution involves altering a model text by changing certain elements of it. Providing students with texts to adapt for themselves can work very well, especially with lower attainers. Model how to spot which words to change and how you would change them for yourself before asking students to do the same thing. An interactive whiteboard is a great tool for making this visually explicit. However, do not hold students back from writing for themselves: if they get too dependent on adapting texts, they will never reach the stage of putting their own sentences together.

In languages where gender and verb forms are more prominent than in English, students need to learn the 'knock on effect' changes have on other elements within the sentence. A good way to practise this is to display a sentence on the board in the target language, change one of its elements and then ask students to identify what other elements now need to be changed. For example, use a sentence like this: I am going to the shop with my little *brother*. Change *brother* to *sister* and ask students to tell you what other words now need to change; continue in this way, changing *shop* to *shops*, *I* to *Frank*, *with* to *without*, and so on. Practice like this helps students to appreciate and understand how to apply what they have learned when writing as well as adapting text.

★ Extended writing

Audience and purpose

Producing 'chunks' of writing which they have put together for themselves is something which students should have the chance to do right from the beginning of their language learning. Flick through a student's exercise book or folder and see what kind of written work you have asked them to do: if the written work is only at word level – grammar exercises, vocabulary copying, substitution exercises – it is likely that the student is not being challenged enough.

When you are setting extended writing tasks, try to give them a clear purpose. At the simplest level, this might be students writing about themselves so that they tell others about their own life. Such tasks become more interesting if you ask students to do the task from the point of view of somebody else, for example, a famous person, a book character or a person from the target language country.

Fairly mundane tasks are enlivened if you ask students to use their imagination: describing their ideal house instead of their own house gives students much more scope to use a range of vocabulary, takes the pressure off those students whose own home circumstances are tricky and gives them the chance to be creative. Inventing and describing a cartoon superhero practises the same language as describing a family member, but helps to engage, motivate and stretch students as they write.

Extended writing does not just mean blocks of text. Students can produce PowerPoint presentations or photo stories with captions. They can write pieces of commentary for pictures or photos on a display board or poems or songs based on a model or idea.

Finally, giving students an audience for their written work helps to motivate and involve them. Establishing a link with a school in the target language country provides an excellent reason for students to produce written work as they know it will be read by their counterparts abroad. Provided it is made anonymous, work can also be posted on the school's virtual learning environment or website with place for comments from other students, parents or any other reader, potentially giving students a worldwide audience for their work! Older students can produce reading material for younger ones to use in class: post-16 students can write readers for Key Stage 3 students, while Key Stage 3 students can produce colourful and interactive readers for primary school learners, based, for example, on an existing well-known children's story which they have analysed and adapted. Producing 'fortune tellers' on folded paper or 'chance cards' for board games which are used in class makes writing have a real purpose.

Approaching extended writing tasks

When you ask students to write something, it is a good idea to make clear what it is you are looking for in the piece of work. You may want students to use a new aspect of grammar which they have just learned, include specific things they have been learning or show how creative they can be. If you have asked them to produce a poster, for example, then presentation and layout might be important. I like to make my success criteria clear by displaying them on the board or at the top of the task.

You can also establish success criteria by getting students to generate them for themselves. You can do this by presenting students with a quality piece of work and asking them to work with a partner to highlight or pick out what it is that makes this a good response. By collecting students' findings together as a class, you can establish a set of success criteria for them to work towards in their own work. With this sort of approach, you can use work from the class or from previous students. If you do, make sure you have asked permission from the student concerned or blanked out the name of the writer if appropriate.

Examination board criteria such as those provided for GCSE or A-level writing help students to recognize what a quality response will look like: personalizing these for specific tasks helps them to understand what these criteria might look like in practice.

Getting students writing
Once you have ensured that students are clear about the audience and purpose of their writing, you can use different ways to help them produce quality written work.

Building on prior knowledge
In pairs or groups, get students to brainstorm the language they already know which they can include in their piece of writing. You can help them structure their thinking by producing or agreeing headings under which they can group key language (e.g. *conditional tense verbs, connectives, opinion phrases*). Students can then work together or as individuals to put together their text.

Writing in pairs
At times, ask students to produce a piece of writing with their partner or group instead of as individuals. The advantage of

writing together is that students talk about what they are going to write and in doing so explain to each other and justify what they think is good to write. Even if a stronger student is the one who actually writes, weaker students can contribute ideas and thoughts on what to include: an important part of the writing process.

Modelling

Modelling is the technique by which you talk through your thinking process as you demonstrate something. The secondary strategy (*Training Materials for the Foundation Subjects* DfES (2002)) highlighted this technique for teachers and made teachers aware of how it can be used effectively in modern languages lessons. When I introduce a writing task, I might begin by modelling to students how I would put together the first part of the work. I write a sentence or two on the board, explaining my thinking (in English) as I go so that students see how I make decisions about what to include, use resources, apply rules and check what I have done. I then bring the class more into the process by asking for suggestions and getting other students to comment, explain and improve what has been suggested, as I gradually write up what is agreed on the board. I then ask the students either to carry on with the writing from where we finished or to produce their own piece of writing, using the sort of thinking which I have modelled.

From dud to dude

This is a technique I like to use to show students how to improve written work. I display a correct but basic paragraph on the board and then ask the students how this could be improved. Using their suggestions, I alter the basic text and make additions so that it becomes more complex. In this way, students begin to understand that it is not just accuracy which makes a good piece of work. Even the least able students can appreciate that they can improve their work by adding, for example, an opinion or two, even if there are quite a few mistakes. Likewise, more able students learn the importance of varying their language and including more complex sentences.

Writing frames

When students are writing in a foreign language, they need to consider both what to write and how to write it. Writing frames help students know what to write as they provide a suggested structure for a piece of work; for example, the content of each paragraph. In a writing frame, you can also include sentence starters and suggested vocabulary or language structures to get students writing. Bear in mind, though, that writing frames should always be a support rather than a constraint: make sure that more able students in particular are not held back in their writing by sticking too closely to a given writing frame.

Supporting independent writing

Having a variety of resources to support students when they are writing helps them to improve the quality of their work. Clear and visible classroom display posters of key verbs, important connectives, quantifiers, and the like, are helpful only if you constantly remind students about them and tell them to use them as they are writing. Of course, if you are not teaching in a modern languages classroom, you will not have this sort of support on hand. Think about making a set of laminated 'self-help' cards which are on the desk for every lesson. These cards can be two sided and contain a variety of vital things which students need when writing, for example, key verbs, past participles, articles, time phrases, connectives. They do not include vocabulary but high frequency language which can be recycled no matter what the topic is. Students find these cards really helpful and get into the habit of using them to embellish their work as well as to make it more accurate. Such a card (or 'placemat') is ideal for supporting differentiation as the least able can use it for support with spelling while the most able can stretch themselves by including a greater range of language.

Drafting and redrafting

There is no point in students completing a draft and then copying up exactly the same thing in their neatest handwriting or on computer, yet, this can sometimes happen when we ask students to do a rough draft of their written work. To avoid this, make sure that there is some sort of peer or self-assessment after the first draft has been produced. Go back to the criteria and ask students to look at their own or each others' work, identifying where the criteria have been met and where they have not. Be specific and ask them, for example, to underline five interesting adjectives, or five past tense verbs, and then check each for accuracy. Peer or self-assessment of written work can be tricky in modern languages as students are not always good at identifying whether something is correct or not. However, all students should be able to have a go at identifying features within the work, even if they are not so good at spotting if the feature is used accurately.

Students need then to be given time to alter and add to their draft so that the final version is an improvement on the original.

Checking written work

Students need to get used to checking that their work makes sense. Get them to read their written work aloud to themselves when they have finished, as this can help them spot missing words. In pairs, students can swap books and choose random sentences from each other's work to translate into English. This process can help students spot missed words or sections which make no sense.

Many students are more than glad to have finished a piece of writing and have no desire to spend any more time looking at it than is strictly necessary! However, students need to learn that systematically checking their work for accuracy is an important aspect of being a language learner. As they get more proficient in their language learning, they need to improve their checking skills. So teach them how to check key aspects relevant to the language you are teaching, such as:

> Nouns: for example, gender/correct article used.
> Adjectives: for example, position/ending.
> Verbs: for example, correct tense used/correct formation.
> Word order: for example, pronouns/verb position.
> Accents: on the letter/correct one used.

To encourage students to develop good checking skills, you can use checklists or prompts. Show them how to look through work once for nouns, then for adjectives, and so on. Another technique is to use a 'checking production line': in groups, students pass their work round each other. Each person in the group has his or her own 'specialist checking area' to look at (e.g. word order) but needs to look at this aspect in everybody's work.

Improving the quality of students' language
Students need to be aware of how to improve their written work by varying their vocabulary and the structures they use. Ideas for working on this in class include the following.

Introducing opposites/synonyms
When you meet and note a new adjective or verb, introduce also the opposite and/or synonyms for that word.

Ladders
Using a picture of a ladder on the board or interactive whiteboard, ask students to place words on an appropriate rung of the ladder depending on how 'fancy' they are.

Rewarding good work
Reward students for good vocabulary use. A young teacher in my area has a hotel reception–type bell on his desk which he pings whenever a student uses a high quality word or structure of his or her own accord.

Using analogies

Use analogies to help students understand what makes good language. For example, refer to structures as 'gold', 'silver' or 'bronze' so that students appreciate what good language is. Ron Wallace of Assessments and Qualification Alliance (AQA) suggests getting students to think of their language stock as a cupboard or larder in which things are arranged on different shelves. Work with students so that they are clear about what kind of structures are on the 'top shelf' and refer to language in this way so that students are encouraged to use 'top shelf language' when they can. Displaying the 'larder' and gradually adding to it as new structures come up will help students embed the language.

Fancy structure cards

When students are working on a task, give out 'fancy structure cards' to specific students. On the card, put the phrase and its meaning, for example, *Having finished my homework, . . .; What I really like is. . . .* Students need to incorporate the phrase they have been given into their work. They should also record the phrase for recycling at a later date.

Using ICT for writing

ICT can enable students who find it difficult to write to put together sentences of their own by choosing and ordering the words they need. Although this is writing based on reading, as they need to know the meaning of the words they see, it nevertheless involves them in being creative and selecting words in order to create something new.

Working on the computer to produce written work enables students to correct and alter what they have written with ease. They can easily insert embellishments into their text in order to improve it. For example, when they have finished their piece of work, you can provide them with a set of time phrases/quantifiers/connectives to insert into what they have written in order to improve the range of language used.

If your students are using computers in class, you may find that you spend a lot of time talking to them about technical ICT-related issues. Instead, try to make sure you take the opportunity to talk to them about their work. Probe their understanding by asking them why they have written certain things and talk through errors with them.

Students can self-assess their work by highlighting verbs or textual features they have used, which makes checking and correction easier. Peer assessment of each others' work can also be done effectively: students can sit in front of a peer's work, and mistakes can be highlighted and comments added easily. Just make sure that students save a copy of their original work as well so that their work is protected from any accidental (or malicious!) deleting by their peer assessor.

I have seen students' GCSE French written work completely ruined as they 'didn't bother to put the accents in'; therefore, not a single past tense verb was correct. Make sure that your students know how to add accents when they are using ICT. Accents can be added through using the *control* and *shift* keys with the accent symbol from the keyboard and the appropriate letter. Alternatively, for accents, umlauts and a range of other characters, students can learn to use *Insert symbol* or the *Alt* key and the appropriate number code.

Finally, what about online resources such as spelling and grammar checkers or online dictionaries? When students are working with computers, such online aids are a mere click away. On the other hand, at present, examination boards have firm rules on what students are allowed to access when preparing work for assessment: you need to check the latest guidance from your examination board. The key seems to be to take a rational approach. Online translators and dictionaries exist, so students are going to need to know about them. You can highlight with students when they are useful (e.g. for looking up words and short phrases) and when they are not (e.g. for translating an essay originally written in English into the target language!). Show students what happens when you take a chunk of an unknown language and put it through the translator into English, so that they appreciate the pitfalls. Also get your students familiar with how to access nuances of meaning through the translator by double checking back from the translation given.

Writing and differentiation

Different sorts of tasks lend themselves to different levels of written response. It is relatively straightforward to set different tasks on a common theme. For example, the less able might be asked to draw and label their favourite meal, while the more able write some sentences about it; similarly, weaker students could write a description of their home town, while the more able can instead explain what they like and dislike about their home town and why. You can ask students to choose which task they will do but you need to keep an eye on their choices and quietly suggest an easier or more challenging task for those who need it.

If you ask all students to do the same written task, for example from a textbook, you can devise your own differentiated success criteria so that students can see what they are aiming for and the most able can stretch themselves. Success criteria can be linked to national curriculum levels, or you can use a 'bronze, silver, gold' or * or ** classification as a guide to the level of challenge. This could be very quickly written on the board as a reminder to students, for example,

* Just write about yourself.

** Write about yourself and one other family member.

Such success criteria can refer not just to content, that is, how much to write and what to include, but also to quality, as in this example from a colleague of mine:

Task: Write about your weekend leisure activities in German.	
*	• Write three or four sentences about what you do at the weekend. • Include time phrases and who you do activities with. • Join your sentences with *and* and *but*. • Check you have used the right verb with each activity.
**	• Write two paragraphs about what you do at the weekend. • Include time phrases, who you do activities with and give opinions on why you enjoy them. • Use *because* as well as *and* and *but*. • Use the pronoun 'wir' as well as 'ich'. Check that your verbs are correct.
***	• Write about what you do at the weekend, writing a paragraph or more for each day. Also give a brief idea of your plans for next weekend. • Include time phrases, who you do activities with and give opinions on why you enjoy them, using a range of connectives to join your sentences. • Use a range of pronouns as well as 'ich' (e.g. er/sie/wir/sie (pl)). • Check all of your verb endings are correct and that you are using the correct tenses (present and future).

Using the target language

Trends and swings in target language use

This chapter is about how best to use the language being taught (i.e. the 'target language') to deliver the lesson itself. Over past years, language teaching in the United Kingdom has tended to swing from one extreme to the other. Twenty years ago, teachers were expected to carry out the whole lesson using the target language. As the focus on assessment for learning and learning how to learn has grown, there has been a tendency to move towards using more English in lessons. However, recent Her Majesty's Inspectorate/the Office of Standards in Education (HMI/OFSTED) reports on modern language teaching in England, such as *Modern Languages: Achievement and Challenge 2007–2010* (2011), have pointed out that there is a real need to develop target language use in modern languages lessons in English schools.

Ironically, target language use tends to lessen rather than grow over the years at secondary school. So while it is quite common for Year 7 (ages 11–12 years) lessons to be carried out almost entirely in the language being learned, as students move up the school, teachers – and students – may tend to use more English.

What is best practice?

Many modern languages teachers have strong beliefs about target language use. There is no doubt that using the target language extensively in lessons can lead to huge benefits for students. Unlike for their counterparts in France, Spain, Portugal or China, our language lesson is likely to be the only chance in a busy week for our students to hear the language being spoken. By being exposed to the language, students become more familiar with the cadences, sound patterns and accents which they need to emulate. Their listening skills develop as they are constantly hearing the language in context and using clues such as facial expression to help them make sense of what is being said. Students are challenged to use higher-order thinking as they need to analyse what they hear and apply their prior knowledge to enable them to understand. They become more confident about dealing with the language they hear because they are used to it, and are relaxed about having to work out meaning. They improve their vocabulary and range of expression. Perhaps most importantly, they see and hear the language being used for the purposes of real communication.

The benefits are therefore crystal clear. However, target language use needs careful planning and management on our part. For some students, the foreign language which they are learning can seem a bit like a nasty monster! If we want students to perceive us as being on *their* side against the 'monster', and not on the side of the 'monster', we need to be careful. It is easy to alienate learners and make them switch off by using the target language extensively with too little support. Likewise, one of the most important aspects of learning is that students feel they have a good relationship with their teacher: it is not easy to establish ideal relationships merely through the target language. Particularly skilful teachers can do this on the basis of their own charisma and personality: for the rest of us, it can be really hard to build individual relationships and a 'we're all in this together' feeling without ever using English. My own view is that a modern languages teacher's use of the target language should be as an aspect of methodology as opposed to an ideology. Using the target language at the expense of students' learning makes no sense.

In summary, the way forward lies in 'fitness for purpose': while aiming to carry out the vast majority of the lesson in the target language, the judicious use of English when appropriate is not a crime. The most important thing is that learners know what is going on, understand what they are learning, are making progress and feel that they are doing so.

To do this successfully, target language use needs to be an integral part of planning, both at a departmental level and when planning individual lessons.

Planning for target language use across the department

It is a good idea to have a policy on target language use in a department so that everybody is clear about expectations within the team. This is important both for continuity between teachers and so that students get a similar quality of experience, no matter who they are taught by. In this policy, you could include the team's philosophy on target language use; how it can be used in the lesson; the precise core language to be used at various stages, both by the teacher and by the students; and what support strategies you will use to make this successful for all learners. Even if you are working on your own on this, you can use a similar approach to plan out how you will try to maximize your use of the target language in your own lessons.

In your planning, you can show how target language use will develop as students grow in confidence. For example, in the first year of language learning, Year 7 (ages 11–12 years), you may choose to present learning objectives in English, both in writing and orally. For the subsequent year group, Year 8 (ages 12–13 years), you may choose to continue to write up your learning objectives in English, but present them verbally in the target language, pointing out the key verbs and phrases on the board as you say them in the target language.

As students progress through the years, you may then decide to present the learning objectives in the target language both orally and in writing, asking students to act as interpreters to ensure they are understood by the whole class. In this way, students gradually build up the language they need for understanding. If you are trying to introduce more extensive target language use with students who are not used to it, then the stages above could be achieved more rapidly.

A similar approach can be taken with the language of task setting. For example, I like to use a 'settling' activity to calm down tricky classes when they enter the room from the lesson before. One task type I use is a matching exercise in which students match up target language words with English ones. The first time I present such an activity, the heading is in English (*Match these up*) together with an image of peas in a pod. I continue to use this template for the next few times I use this activity. I then retain exactly the same template but take out the English words and replace them with a target language version. Students are so used to the activity type and the visual layout that they get straight on with the task instead of clamouring *What do we have to do?*

For which aspects of learning can the teacher use the target language?

As students' linguistic abilities increase over time, the answer to this question is, in fact, all aspects! But here are some suggestions as to possible areas of focus.

★ *Greetings*

Greeting students as they come into the classroom gets the lesson off to a language-focused start. Do not worry if they do not all answer you back: at least they are hearing the target language. Vary your greetings so that they become used to and assimilate a whole range (e.g. hi, hello, good afternoon).

★   *Day-to-day comments*

Comments to students as they enter the classroom or at the end of the lesson can help you recycle language and/or use learned language in a new context. By asking the class how they are or commenting on the weather, you are also using what they have learned for real purposes. By asking students what lesson they have next, for example, you are getting them to begin to understand questions about future events. By asking them what lesson they have just had, they are hearing the past tense used in context.

★   *Taking the register*

If you take a formal register of your classes, you can ensure the class becomes familiar with common structures (e.g. *Where is . . .?*). They can begin to hear how questions are formulated (e.g. *Is Tom absent?*) and perhaps how adjectives work (e.g. *Is Lucy absent?*). Social conventions can become established (e.g. in French, *Oui, madame* as opposed to merely *Oui*).

★   *Classroom routines*

By using the target language to give classroom instructions, you are making your students receptive to a variety of imperative forms (e.g. *come in, work with a partner*). They begin to hear the difference when you address the whole class and when you address individuals. Classroom objects can be recapped early in the course together with key phrases such as *I haven't got . . ., I've forgotten . . .* By using these phrases in class, students practise grammatical skills such as substitution and using the correct article (e.g. *a/the/my*) in real contexts.

★   *Setting up activities*

Coupled with plenty of visual support (see below), activities such as reading tasks, listening activities or games can be set up and explained using the target language (e.g. *copy the grid, write 1–10*). The key is to think carefully about the words you will choose to use and how you are going to support these words.

★ *Classroom management*

Basic classroom management can take place in the target language (e.g. *You have 5 seconds to get ready: 5 . . . 4 . . . 3 . . . 2 . . . 1 . . . OK!*) It is important to remember the principles of positive behaviour management when using the target language (e.g. using *thank you* instead of *please* when making a request; drawing attention to good behaviour rather than criticizing bad behaviour).

★ *Grammar and knowledge about language*

Grammar teaching is often an area for which teachers feel that the use of English is more apt so that students gain a clear understanding of what is being learned. Nevertheless, setting learning objectives in the target language allows students to gain a passive knowledge of verbs to do with learning and progress (e.g. *to use; to understand*). These verbs are useful when students are discussing their progress or setting targets later in their school life. Simple grammatical terms are often similar words in the target language and English (e.g. noun, verb, feminine). Teaching students these words enables you to use them when talking about sentences or taking feedback from exercises.

Supporting your use of the target language

Students can so easily be switched off learning if they are hit by a barrage of language which they perceive they cannot understand. One of the things which stops students behaving well and focusing in language lessons can be that they are set a task but then insist they do not know what to do. Sometimes this is because the target language has been used without the relevant back up to ensure understanding.

If you are trying to increase the quality and quantity of your target language input, you need to develop a range of strategies to ensure that this is successful.

★ Chunking the lesson

When you have planned your lesson, use a highlighter pen to highlight which parts you are going to conduct in the target language. This should be blocks of time. It is more effective and less confusing for students to have large chunks in the target language rather than you chopping and changing as you go. For parts of the lesson when you do want to use English, flag this up to your students in the target language: *Now I am going to speak in English for a while.* This helps you avoid 'parrot syndrome', when you find yourself saying a sentence in the target language then repeating it afterwards in English. Sometimes, this can happen almost subconsciously, but if done consistently, students quickly learn that there is no real incentive to listen the first time.

★ Using visual support

Providing visual support is vital when explaining tasks and exercises, particularly to support the less able. If you want your class to draw a grid, draw it yourself or have 'one you did earlier' to display as you describe what students have to do. If you want students to respond to a listening task in English, provide them with an example on the board as you explain. This enables students to access what they have to do, even if they have not understood your instructions.

★ Face and gesture

As in real life, a facial expression or a gesture can really help your students to understand what you want them to do. Sometimes, modern languages teachers can look a bit like puppets, nodding, shaking their heads, and gesturing whenever possible! But miming verbs out or using gestures to indicate what students should do is a simple way to avoid the use of English while ensuring your students know what to do.

★ *Careful word choice*

Of all the support you can give your students, choosing your words carefully is probably the most effective way to ensure you do not lose them along the way. Conversely to what one might imagine, I sometimes find I am more effective at using the target language when teaching my second foreign language rather than my first, as I really do have to think about the words I choose to use and prepare what I am going to say. If we are at total ease when speaking the language, we may find that we say just a little too much more than is actually needed and therefore do not take the students with us. So making sure that our instructions or questions are clear and to the point is important. If relevant to the language you are teaching, making full use of cognates can help students to latch on to what we are saying. If we want students to describe something in French, for example, we need to choose our words carefully: *Décris-moi . . .* requires prior knowledge, while *Fais-moi la description de . . .* gives students the chance to work out what you might be saying.

★ *Ensuring comprehension*

After explaining a task or an activity in the target language, one way of checking that the class has understood is through thumbs up/thumbs down: you can ask the question *Have you understood?* and show students how to express *yes* or *no* by using gesture. You can ask the question *Who has understood?* and get one student to act as an interpreter for the rest of the class by explaining in English to the others.

With all these supporting techniques, the support can and should be withdrawn gradually so that students become increasingly independent over time.

Getting students to use the target language

It is one thing for the teacher to use the target language as much as he or she can: it is quite another for the students to answer spontaneously and use the target language among themselves for normal classroom business. We should not feel too bad if students are doing more listening than responding: after all, through listening, they are building up their receptive skills and will be responding in other ways than verbally, for example, doing what is asked of them. Nevertheless, it is important that you make clear to your students why they need to talk in the target language whenever they can. If students believe in the importance of taking risks, contributing and trying to say things, they will try to do it. If they perceive using the target language as part and parcel of lessons to be artificial and pointless, they will not make the effort to do so.

Classroom posters with pictures and key phrases help students to remember these (e.g. *can we . . .? have you got . . .?*) and provide a handy reference point. If a student needs to use one of the phrases but says it in English, you can simply point to the poster, thus avoiding the need to use English yourself. Making your posters generic rather than specific (i.e. *may I . . .?* rather than *may I go to the toilet?*) encourages students to see the transferability of phrases across different contexts, and helps them to be more spontaneous in their speech.

Some teachers have a points or tally system which rewards students for making a contribution in the target language. A student can take charge of awarding a point to anyone who contributes. If you adopt such a system, make sure it is used to reward spontaneous target language contributions rather than participation in normal classwork: the latter should be an expectation of all students.

Another successful tactic is to allow students to call out or comment on the lesson as long as they do so in the target language. This allows students to practise their opinion words and agreeing/disagreeing phrases in a real context, and they thrive on the chance to make spontaneous comments.

Some teachers insist on students using the target language for the whole lesson or have blocks of time when students are only allowed to use the target language. This might include during a pair-work activity, for example. Bear in mind that it is always better to reward those who do speak the language than punish those who do not. Adapting a technique suggested by Dylan Wiliam, you might like to secretly decide on a 'mystery student'. The student does not know who he or she is, but you secretly observe him or her to see if he or she manages to speak no English during the specified time. If so, the whole class is told who the student is and rewarded. If not, the class is not rewarded but does not find out who the 'mystery student' was.

While it is a good idea to have a planned structure for target language use, you also need to try to be flexible. It can be a unifying factor for a class to have its own 'bank' of target language which has been developed over the weeks as situations have arisen. So if some students are late for class because they spilled some acid in science, do not shy away from giving them the words they need to express this. If you can do so without losing pace, you can write up words or phrases as they crop up, thereby helping to build and reinforce your students' range of vocabulary.

For some activities, you need to weigh up carefully the learning involved versus student target language use to decide where your emphasis will lie. Peer assessment is a good example of this. You can create tick lists using symbols and simple language which allow students to look at (or listen to) each others' work and provide feedback to each other through the target language. However, if your focus is on developing your students' analysis and evaluation skills as well as their ability to give clear and useful feedback, it may well be more effective to get them to assess each other in English. Of course, over time, your ultimate aim will be to build up the language students need to be able to express their thinking effectively in the target language. Nevertheless, I would rather see and hear students using English to discuss and analyse work against the examination board GCSE criteria than doing a more superficial analysis merely in order to use the target language.

Grammar, thinking and creativity 8

How do grammar, thinking and creativity link together?

In the past, language teaching in the United Kingdom, especially for younger students, has sometimes been about learning chunks of ready-made language without really knowing the underlying story of how it all fits together to make sense. Such an approach relies heavily on memory: if you can't remember what you have learned, or indeed did not learn it properly in the first place, then you are stuck.

It is true that examination specifications, such as that for the current GCSE examination, include a list of grammar to be taught. However, when the students are actually examined, they can get good grades even if they have not really understood grammar rules nor have applied them for themselves to any great extent. This gives us a justification for shying away from grammar teaching and focusing on the acquisition of vocabulary and structures.

However, by exposing students to grammar and patterns, and giving them practice in applying these rules and patterns, we help them to learn to think about the language and how it works. This in turn gives students the capability of being creative, by which in this context we mean nothing more than being able to put words together to say what they want to say.

We also need to remember that understanding how the language works helps to make modern languages a viable subject on the curriculum. Back in the 1950s, Bloom researched and analysed thousands of questions asked by teachers. One result of this research is a taxonomy or classification system (known as Bloom's Taxonomy) which can be used to categorize the levels of thinking we ask students to use in the classroom. In terms of Bloom's Taxonomy, recall and comprehension represent the lowest level of challenge. Bloom's higher-order categories of thinking include application, analysis, synthesis and evaluation. Grammar is one area which brings our subject as a discipline in line with other subjects, as students are required to develop their thinking through application, analysis and synthesizing what they have learned to produce something new.

Sometimes teachers avoid teaching grammar because it can seem dull and uninspiring. Grammar is also a difficult area for students as they are required to use higher-order thinking skills and grasp concepts and ideas which may be quite alien to them, such as gender or case systems. As with other aspects of teaching modern languages, all depends on the approach taken and the amount of student involvement in the learning process. In much the same way as students learn to tackle abstract concepts and logical rules in subjects like mathematics, we should not shy away from working with students of all abilities to gain the building blocks they need to be able to do something with the language they are learning. The thinking skills they use in the process can be practised, developed and used in other subject areas as well as in their daily lives.

Teaching grammar

★ *When to teach grammar*

There are different approaches to deciding when to teach aspects of grammar. Grammar points can be tackled as and when they arise in texts or as they are needed for certain tasks. Alternatively, grammatical progression can lie at the heart of the scheme of work, with texts, topics and tasks chosen to highlight and practise the grammar in question. Your scheme of work or textbook will probably follow one of these approaches and help you know when to focus on different aspects of grammar.

Whatever approach is chosen, try to ensure that the new grammar has been met in context before any 'dissection' takes place. But grammar needs to be explicitly taught, practised, revisited and applied so that students see its importance and are able to manipulate the language for themselves. If an aspect of grammar is key to progression, make it the focus of your lesson rather than an aside or an add-on. An effective learning objective for your lesson will often have grammar, rather than the topic or theme you are working on, at its heart, and will be transferable to other contexts (see Chapter 2).

When you work on a grammar point in modern languages lessons, the current learning sometimes seems to block out everything else the students have learned; for example, if students study reflexive verbs in French, German or Spanish, suddenly *every* verb they write seems to come with a reflexive pronoun attached! Two things are important here: first, ensuring that grammar points are revisited in your lessons over time so that students do not forget them; and second, once new grammar is embedded, making sure that you mix up what students work on so that they become used to seeing and using different forms within the same piece of work.

★ Grammatical terminology

Do not be afraid to use the technical terminology of grammar in learning objectives and explanations: students should be used to this from their English lessons and hearing terminology reused in their modern languages lessons will help to reinforce what they have learned elsewhere. Most importantly, this will provide you and your class with a common shorthand vocabulary to talk about language, learning and progress. Learners are expected to cope with technical language and subject-specific vocabulary in their other subjects.

Even our youngest students need to build with our help an understanding of terms such as *noun, verb, pronoun, gender, tense, infinitive, ending,* as well as other terminology key to specific languages, for example *subject/object* for German, or *preterite* for Spanish. To reach this understanding, you can make links with English and practise identifying examples of different aspects of grammar (e.g. nouns, past tenses) in English before applying them to target language examples.

As many grammatical terms tend to be cognates or quite easily recognizable, over time, you can build up your students' understanding and use of the target language when talking about grammar. This could start off as simply as looking at nouns on the board and asking in French, for example, *'C'est masculin ou féminin?'* Students will quickly latch on to using the gender terms themselves in their responses. Gradually building in target language grammatical terminology to your scheme of work will help you to increase your own expectations and your students' prowess.

★ *Approaches to teaching grammar*

Research into how we learn best tells us that learning through discussion and 'doing' leads to better retention rates than learning through lecture or audiovisual presentation. In other words, working things out for yourself helps you to remember them better too. Bearing this in mind when approaching the teaching of grammar will help you to plan effective ways of getting your students to understand how the language works. There are plenty of fancy PowerPoint presentations available on the internet that introduce grammar points with sound, music and lots of animation. But ultimately, these can merely serve as an audiovisual presentation in which students are shown how the grammar point works and then asked to apply it.

Whenever you meet or are teaching a new grammar point, try to use as your guiding principle that you will ask the students to work out for themselves what the rule is. Often ready-made resources can be 'tweaked' or adapted to change the focus away from 'showing' or 'telling' to letting students discover things for themselves: sometimes, this is just a matter of omitting things or changing the order of a set of PowerPoint slides.

You may feel that lower-attaining students will not respond to this kind of work. Start on a small scale, and set tasks up as a puzzle or 'investigation'. A former colleague would don a white lab coat when presenting 'CSI Language' tasks to her classes!

Building on prior knowledge

On a day-to-day basis, try to get into the habit of asking students to work out or speculate on how new grammatical features might work. At the simplest level, this can be encouraged through questioning: if you meet the feminine form of an adjective in a text, ask the students to try to tell you what they think the masculine form might be; if you meet a new verb, ask them to try to work out what they think the past participle could be. This sort of questioning needs you to use speculative language (e.g. 'What do you think *might* happen if . . .?') so that students are encouraged to think and experiment with patterns. Make sure that the students have the chance to think in pairs so that they talk to each other about the possibilities. Similarly, if you meet a new verb, give students all the parts of the verb on the board or on cards and ask them to see how far they can get with reconstructing the paradigm by matching the verb parts with pronouns. This will help them build up their ability to think in patterns and look for commonalities.

Inductive grammar teaching

One effective approach to teaching grammar is the following sequence:

- Students meet examples of the grammatical feature.
- Students analyse and try to formulate rules.

- Students present and discuss how robust their rule is.
- The rule is refined.
- The rule is noted.
- The rule is practised.
- The rule is applied in new contexts.

I like to have examples of a grammatical feature on pieces of card so that students can physically group and easily rearrange the cards as they look for patterns. Alternatively, examples of the grammatical feature can be presented through a text which students are asked to highlight. You can also present the grammar point in context orally, using visuals with your presentation to help students grasp meaning. For example, a picture of somebody dreaming can help you introduce conditional tense phrases such as *I would like . . ., I would have . . .* and *I would be . . .*

Once students have met the examples, this sort of technique is most effective when students are in pairs or groups so that they can discuss possibilities and agree or disagree with each other. You can ask one pair or group to present its initial thoughts to the rest of the class, then get others to contribute and build on their thoughts until an appropriate explanation has been agreed.

When students do activities in which they are required to analyse rather than understand the meaning of language, they find it hard to ignore meaning and just look at 'form'. A good analogy is with cryptic crosswords: if you try to work out a clue through mere meaning, you will get nowhere! Students need to learn how to look at the words in an almost mathematical way. Indeed, this can be a helpful way of looking at grammar for students: just like in a maths calculation, there is usually only one right answer as far as grammar is concerned.

Less able students also need to be encouraged to use and develop their higher-level thinking skills through working with grammar and sentence structure. Which is 'easier': trying to recall the meaning of a set of words you have been taught or trying to puzzle out what patterns you can see with a partner?

By asking students to think in this way, we can help them to get better at this sort of analytical thinking and therefore help them to become both better linguists and better learners.

When students are doing this sort of thinking, they are talking in English. For me, the benefit of such an approach outweighs the fact that part of the lesson is in English, as students tend to get involved and learn better than they otherwise would.

Making things physical

When teaching grammar, physical props or getting students to move around are helpful methods for increasing students' understanding and making the lesson come alive. You can use the interactive whiteboard to demonstrate how endings change or word order alters as the words or letters can be physically moved around by you or a student. Big word cards or cards with parts of words on (e.g. verb stems and endings) act as a visual hook to aid explanations. Getting students to hold these cards and arrange themselves so that they are in the correct order is an effective way to illustrate the cause-and-effect nature of grammar. To save time in producing lots of resources, you can use mini-whiteboards for activities like this, getting students in groups to write a word each on their whiteboard and using these instead of cards.

Using analogies

Drawing analogies with things with which students are familiar helps them to understand how grammar works. Students are also good at coming up with their own analogies. For example:

- In French, teaching negatives as 'the *ne ... pas* sandwich', with the verb as the filling;
- In German, teaching subordinating conjunctions as 'verb kickers', which kick the verb to the end of the clause;
- Using a flower stem with petals to illustrate a verb stem and possible endings.

Comparison with English

Do not be afraid to make direct comparison between English and the grammar of the language you are teaching. This will help students to begin to understand that producing their own sentences is not about translating word by word, but involves a filtering stage; for example, translating *I am going* needs the learner to think '*I am going* is the present tense; how do I say the present tense of the verb *to go* in the target language?' Model this by talking through your own thought processes when you are producing language. This will help students to see how they need to think.

Practising grammar

Grammar practice does not need to be dull. Once the pattern or rule is clear, practice is a vital stage before students can apply rules in context.

★   Individual grammar exercises

There are plenty of grammar practice exercises in textbooks and online. These are useful for classwork and homework practice. Use time limits to make things snappy and do not feel students should always be working in silence: if they discuss their answers, they may increase their understanding. It is a good idea to get students to mark each others' work as soon as the task is completed so that they get immediate feedback while the task is still fresh in their minds.

As students work on such tasks, walk round the class asking individuals to justify and explain what they have written. This will encourage them to really understand what they are doing rather than work through it mechanically. Ask students who finish the task quickly to come up with some additional examples of the grammar exercise for another quick finisher to complete.

★ *Whole class grammar practice*

For grammar practice exercises as a whole class, it is again a good idea to use mini-whiteboards, or have a series of options on which students vote. This allows you to gauge students' levels of understanding. Game show formats such as 'Who Wants to be a Millionaire?' are ideal for this. You can choose options which really get to the heart of students' understanding. For example, in German, the question 'How do you say *I went*?' could have the following options:

a. *ich gehen*: If chosen, the student has not yet got the concept of the infinitive and how it needs to change;
b. *ich gegangen*: If chosen, the student has not yet got the idea of the perfect tense having two parts;
c. *ich habe gegangen*: If chosen, the student is getting the idea of perfect tense formation, but has forgotten that this verb is an exception, that is, goes with *sein*;
d. *ich bin gegangen*: If not chosen, do some students think this means *I am going*?

The pace of the game needs to be maintained, but careful questioning after each option will help to clarify students' understanding.

★ *Correct the mistake*

Some teachers feel that this is not a good technique as students see incorrect forms. However, how can students learn to check work for errors if they have not had practice in doing this? Use a heading or image which reminds students that this is a 'correct the mistake' exercise. Within the exercise, keep your mistakes to the grammatical point the students are studying but vary the type of error to ensure a deeper understanding.

★ *Producing grammar machines and devices*

I have worked with imaginative teachers who have asked their students to produce a range of devices to practice grammar. For example, to practise a compound tense (e.g. the perfect tense in French or German), use the inside of a toilet roll with another cardboard roll around it. The outer roll is cut up into three so that each piece can rotate independently around the core. The first part has the personal pronouns written around it in the target language; the middle section has the parts of the verb *to have* and/or *to be* and the third section has a selection of past participles. Students are given a past tense verb in English and must align the three sections of their roll to form the verb in the target language. This sort of approach helps students to understand that the tense has three parts which must fit together to produce the one correct answer. They enjoy physically producing and then moving the device as well, which helps to consolidate the concepts.

You can ask students to design and make a machine or device to practise any grammar point. They can produce this and others can test it out. The time spent on designing the machine will help them to reach a deeper understanding of the grammatical feature and how it works. The time spent on actually producing the device needs to be tightly limited, however!

★ *Using dice*

Dice are a handy tool for practising grammar orally as they introduce an element of randomness which requires a certain amount of spontaneity. You can buy or make big dice and stick different things on each face or you can use normal dice and give each number an option. Dice are especially good for practising verbs, as working in pairs or small groups, students can practise verbs with different pronouns or with different tenses according to the roll of the dice. To make things interesting, you can have something different if a six is rolled; for example, they need to do all the tenses, or they can choose the pronoun they want.

★ *Other grammar games*

Common games can be adapted for practising grammar, for example:

- Noughts and crosses.
- Randomizer: use a randomizer on the computer to throw up random pronouns and get students to decline a key verb accordingly.
- Throwing the ball: say a pronoun, throw the ball, ask the student to say the correct form of the verb back to you, continue in pairs.
- Odd-one-out.
- Consequences.
- 'I went to market'.
- Battleships.
- Dominoes.

★ *Chants and songs*

Set verbs to the music of well-known songs or ask your students to come up with a rhythmic chant or rap to help them remember rules. Students have enjoyed my collection of French verb football chants as they are set to the 'tune' of well-known chants from the stadium and help them to fix the verbs in their minds.

Being creative with language: Doing a lot with a little

When learners have the basic 'tools' of grammar and understand how sentences fit together, they can be creative with language because they can say what they want to say. The key lies in teaching them how to recycle language in different contexts so that they see how to apply certain key structures in a variety of ways.

★ *Effective use of resources*

Students will only reuse the grammar they have learned if they have the means to readily access it to refresh their understanding. Textbooks usually have a straightforward and relevant grammar section at the back, but how many students actually make use of it? Make sure your students know what is in the grammar section and how to use it. Do some practice activities by getting them to work in pairs to find verb forms by using the verb tables, for example.

Students also need to make sure that they are able to readily access what they need in their own exercise books or files. It is important that students at all levels have legible and specific grammar notes covering the key learning points. Sometimes students' books can get all mixed up, with ephemeral material like listening tasks muddled in with essentials like grammar notes. Get into the habit of asking your students to record grammar notes in a set place where they can easily be located. You could suggest they make an index so that they can quickly find what they need or get them to use a specific highlighter colour to mark up all essential grammar notes. A colleague of mine uses the term 'recycling book' for the notebook in which her students record vocabulary and grammar: a good way of helping students see what they can use the notebook for.

★ *Using plenaries to encourage recycling*

Use plenaries during or at the end of the lesson to encourage students to look across topic boundaries and see how what they have learned can be applied in another context. For example, you can put the key structure in the middle of a spider with six or eight legs and ask the class to work in pairs to complete the sentence (orally or in writing) in different ways. You can also ask the class how they could use the structure they have learned in another situation, for example, in a bank/when chatting with an exchange partner/in a narrative about a wizard/in an argumentative essay.

★ Some creative recycling opportunities

Being silly with content

Amusing or silly examples are more fun to produce and also tend to stick in the mind. For example, to use the present and past tenses together, students can produce sentences like *Normally I have tea and toast for breakfast but yesterday I had a car tyre with blood.* The key language – the verbs – is being recycled, but students are able to be creative within a set framework.

Using drama techniques or role play

Potentially dull topics like 'At the doctors' or 'At the Tourist Information Office' are enlivened if you build in humour. Just providing a title can be enough, for example, 'The Daft Doctor' (who might prescribe cigarettes for tummy ache and tomato soup for toothache) or 'Dullsville Tourist Office' (where the top attraction is the public toilet, perhaps). Students will still be using the structures you want them to use, but the context is engaging and enlivening.

Being somebody else

Writing or speaking as somebody else gives students the chance to recycle their language creatively in a new context. They can write from the point of view of a famous person, a rich spoiled child, a historical character or as somebody from the target language country. An interesting stimulus, such as a weird or unusual picture, can start students thinking and generating ideas. As a result, they are more motivated to write or speak and are able to include more interesting content. Talking about daily life becomes much more interesting if the stimulus is a picture of an alien planet or a child labourer from Sénégal. Objects such as a pipe or an unusual shoe can make creating descriptions of people much more stimulating as students can use their imaginations.

Writing poems or songs

At the simplest level, this could involve a song or model poem in which students replace one noun with another to make it their own, for example,

> *I like* sun, *I hate* rain;
> *I like* smiles, *I hate* frowns.

Even at this level, students are able to put some of their self into the writing, and each person's response will be different. Yes, they will have to use dictionaries, but only to look up nouns, which is something they need to learn to do and practise.

Students will be familiar with certain poetical forms from their English lessons. You could get them writing haikus: three-line poems with five syllables in the first line, seven in the middle line and five in the third line, for example,

> Dance is my passion.
> I turn, I leap, I stand still.
> I am like the wind.

Share some examples with them which you have made up yourself, or from the internet, then let them experiment.

Assessment and progression 9

Why assess our students?

There are practical reasons for assessing our students on a regular basis: as teachers, we need to check how well our students are doing against their capabilities; we need to be able to tell the school and the parents how individuals are progressing; and we need to measure students' progress against national standards so that employers and others know the level they have reached. But above all of this, we need to assess students to enable them to get better. If we do not know how well they are doing, and if *they* do not know what they are good at and how to improve, then students will not make the progress of which they are capable. We need to keep this principle in mind whenever we are talking about assessment, as without it, assessment becomes a mere measuring tool.

A great deal of research has been undertaken on assessment and the work of Black and Wiliam in this area has been very influential (see *Inside the Black Box*, Black and Wiliam (1998)). Understanding terms like 'assessment for learning', 'summative assessment' and 'formative assessment' and how they apply to modern languages will help you to plan assessment more effectively into your lessons. Summative assessment is assessing students at a given moment in time through a test, examination or specific piece of work. Formative assessment involves students getting feedback on their progress during everyday lessons and acting on it. Formative assessment is also referred to as 'assessment for learning': it is not an optional extra or a 'bolt on', but something which needs to be a feature of all lessons. Many features of assessment for learning – such as sharing learning objectives and outcomes, modelling, and sharing success criteria – have already been looked at in previous chapters as they are part and parcel of excellent teaching and learning.

From working with students, I know that they can feel somewhat overwhelmed by assessment in modern languages lessons, perceiving that they are constantly being 'tested'. At the same time, students also tend to say that they do not get enough feedback on how to improve; for example, they do badly in a listening test on a given topic, but do not really see how that connects to the rest of their learning, or how they can improve next time.

Keeping a balance between formative and summative assessment will help you make assessment both a manageable and a worthwhile part of your language lessons. Developing a balanced approach to assessment, with your eye firmly fixed on helping your students to improve, is what this chapter will help you to do.

National assessment schemes

Language teachers have traditionally assessed their students in the four language skills: listening, speaking, reading and writing. The current National Curriculum uses these four skills as the four attainment targets. Students' progress in each of these areas is measured against eight level descriptors which describe what a student can do.

An alternative grading system developed in England is the Languages Ladder, which is a national scheme designed to measure progress in a given language 'from cradle to grave'. The Languages Ladder is based on the Common European Framework, a set of language competences used across Europe to measure capability in languages. Like the National Curriculum, the Languages Ladder provides a way of measuring what people can do in the four language skills.

Modern languages departments in English schools tend to assess their younger students using National Curriculum levels, as this fits in with other subjects and the system is familiar to both students and parents. Some people prefer the more simple 'can do' nature of the Languages Ladder statements. Broadly speaking, the levels of the Languages Ladder equate to those of the National Curriculum, so the two systems are compatible.

When working with National Curriculum levels or other such criteria, it is important to remember that the descriptors refer to what a student can do. Individual pieces of work or tasks can be given a numerical level and this can be used as *evidence* that the student is working at that level, but the real point of the levels is to help you come to an overall 'best fit' judgement: you need to ask yourself 'On the basis of the evidence I have, at what level in each skill is this student operating?' The best way of coming to this judgement is through a balance of summative tasks and your own knowledge of that student's progress in class over time. For example, a piece of written work can be evidence that a student is working at Level 5 or 6, even if it does not contain a range of tenses (part of the descriptor for these levels); over time, however, you will need to be sure, through other pieces of work, that tense use is within the student's capabilities. Similarly, the use of connectives to join up sentences is not mentioned in the National Curriculum levels until Level 7: that does not mean that a student linking his or her sentences with *and* and *but* is already there!

The progress of students studying for GCSE, A-level or other qualifications is measured against a set of grade criteria published by the examination board in question. The Languages Ladder deals with competency to degree level and beyond; therefore, it can provide a useful assessment tool for post-16 students.

The assessment systems above tend to deal with competency or 'performance' in the target language, that is to say outcomes. What 'ladder'-like systems like these do not always take into account is how well your students' development and understanding of concepts, language learning skills and intercultural understanding are progressing. This is another reason why ongoing, day-to-day assessment of progress throughout your lessons is a vital aspect of what we mean when we talk about assessment.

Planning for effective assessment

Assessment needs to be built into your scheme of work in a systematic way. Different schools take different approaches. Textbooks generally come with end-of-unit tests which some schools use religiously, gathering a set of scores which are then translated into levels and grades. Such an approach can become onerous for staff and students alike: too much potential learning time may be squandered on testing; students may feel that they are tested much more in modern languages than in other subjects; teacher time spent in correcting tests may not have enough of an impact on students' learning; and performance in these tests may not reflect a student's actual capabilities.

Another approach is to agree certain tasks which will be done during the course of the year and use these for assessment purposes. These might be tasks from the textbook, tasks you have produced yourself, classwork or homework tasks. I try to make sure that I have recorded students' progress in each of the four skills three or four times in the course of the year, so that I have a picture of their capabilities and how they are doing. The tasks set are marked or graded but as they are part and parcel of daily lessons, it is easier to build them into the teaching programme and help students learn from them. It is helpful to keep separate records of progress in each skill. I like to divide up my mark book into different sections so that I can see at a glance how often I have recorded evidence of progress in each skill for each student.

Assessing speaking

Assessing students' oral work can feel like a huge task. How on earth can you get a real idea of students' ability when you have 30 students to listen to?

I have found the easiest and most successful way to do this on a day-to-day basis is through asking students to work together in pairs. When students are working on an oral task, go around the class and listen to a certain number of students as they talk. Use the relevant grade or National Curriculum level criteria to gain evidence for those students of how their spoken work is coming on, which you can record in your mark book. During each lesson you can try to focus on a different group of students so that, over time (e.g. over the course of the term), you have recorded how well every student is doing in his or her speaking. During the next term, you can try to repeat the process so that by the end of the year you have formally recorded a student's progress on at least three occasions. Using grade or National Curriculum level criteria to assess students means that you do not need to hear them all performing an identical task.

Even if you want to assess all students through the same task, again, most speaking tests or tasks can be assessed in pairs. You can ask pairs to put their hands up when they are ready for you to come to hear them, and provide the class with work to do when they have been listened to. This can work well but can also be exhausting as you dash around trying to fit everybody in. Some teachers call students up individually for an oral test as the classwork on something else. This gives you the chance to focus on one particular student, but students can get nervous and the process can become an ordeal as opposed to part and parcel of your everyday work. For me, a more useful approach is to assess students' speaking as part of a carousel lesson, when students take it in turns to work with you in small groups. In this way, you can have individual interactions with all students for a short period of time as they work with you.

Sometimes, you may wish to assess students making presentations or giving a talk. Again, this can be done effectively in small groups with students presenting to three or four others. If students address the whole class, make sure that everybody is involved by asking the class to assess aspects of the presentation they are listening to.

Finally, digital technology offers some great opportunities for students to record their own oral work for you to assess. On a practical basis, get yourself and your class very well organized so that there are clear systems for naming and sending you files of oral work. As you listen to each student, make a note of what is good and what can be improved so that the student has some concrete feedback on his or her work, which will help him or her to improve next time. Remember that such an approach is extremely time consuming, so use it judiciously.

Practical techniques for effective marking

It is very easy for any teacher to get bogged down with marking and modern languages teachers are no different. The development of a range of techniques to make your marking more worthwhile will not only help your students to learn better but also help you have a life of your own! Modern languages departments should have a marking policy which sets out how and why teachers mark so this is plain to students, colleagues and parents.

★ *Use levels and grades judiciously*

As Black and Wiliam demonstrated in their influential work *Inside the Black Box* (2006), as soon as students' work is given a numerical total or graded, students tend to ignore any written comment or feedback. If you give a specific piece of work a National Curriculum level or grade as part of your ongoing assessment, then do not waste your time providing a detailed comment. Instead, earmark certain pieces of work or tasks for which you will provide quality feedback (verbal or written), which will really help your students improve.

★ Do not mark to check that work has been done

Collecting in piles of books or scrolling through emails simply to check that classwork or homework has been done is time consuming and ineffective. Instead, ask students to hold up their books at the start of the lesson to show you their work so that you can see immediately who has not done what has been set. Alternatively, set the class a task, then walk around the room quickly checking that each student has done the work, ticking or initializing books as you go. You may then correct the task as a class, but students still know that you are aware of who has not done the work as asked.

★ Use peer marking

Peer marking is not peer assessment (see below). It is simply asking students to swap books or papers and correct each others' work. Any finite task with written answers can easily be marked in this way. Life is too short to take home sets of books in order to mark listening and reading tasks, for example. Many such tasks are answered with short responses and can be quickly marked against a set of answers which you provide. Moreover, it is much more beneficial to the students to have immediate feedback on their work: getting a marked set of answers back a week later will not mean a lot to them. Vocabulary tests, grammar exercises, gap-fill tasks and drill exercises can also be marked against an answer scheme so that students can quickly see what they have got wrong and then talk about why.

On the whole, I find that students are very good at doing this fairly, even younger students. Sometimes, teachers worry that students might make a mistake in their marking or just plain cheat! In the big scheme of things, when weighed against the advantages of student self-correction, any small anomalies are simply not worth losing sleep over. If you suspect malpractice, spot check peer marking on a regular basis so that you keep an eye on things.

It is, of course, important for you to keep track of how students are doing and for students to see that you are aware of their progress. Following a self-marked activity, once the students are working on the next task, I often walk around the class and gather students' marks for my mark book, asking individuals for their score using the target language. To acknowledge very good work or effort, I sometimes walk around and use an ink stamp on a student's work, or quickly tick and write an encouraging single-word target language comment.

★ Stagger your marking load

As modern languages teachers, our biggest traditional marking load comes from marking extended oral or written work. Students' ability to produce sentences and chunks of speech or writing for themselves needs to be assessed and monitored by you so that you can see where their strengths and weaknesses are. Rather than have all your classes producing an extended piece for marking at the same time, stagger the bigger pieces over the course of the term across your classes so that you are not left with several classes to mark on the same evening.

★ Target your marking on those who need it

All students need to feel that their efforts are acknowledged over time. That does not mean that everything they do needs to be marked. A teacher I know has three trays at the front of her room. At the end of a lesson, students place their exercise books into the tray of their choice: the green tray is for students who feel they have understood the work well; the orange tray is for those who are not sure that they have understood and the red tray is for those who have really struggled with the work. The teacher then focuses her marking on the red and orange boxes so that those students are given the feedback they need to move their learning on.

★ *Focus your marking*

When marking written work in modern languages, try to make sure that you are marking, not proofreading. Be very clear about what you are looking for in the piece of work, and share this with the students. As a result of this clarity, focus your marking and do not necessarily correct every error you see. I have worked with several colleagues in the past, particularly native speakers, who have gasped in horror at the idea of letting mistakes go uncorrected! Indeed, in some cases, this will be inappropriate, for example, when students are later going to reproduce their writing from memory, or when you are dealing with advanced or high achieving students who should be making very few errors. In general, however, the amount of time you spend on correcting every error is better spent on focused marking followed by a personal comment which points out exactly what was done well and how to improve.

If your department does adopt a policy of not correcting every error, be sure that the rationale for this is made explicit to students, parents and leadership teams so that they do not think laziness is the reason for errors being left uncorrected!

★ *Use peer assessment before you correct extended work*

If you make your success criteria clear to students, you can ask them to check their own or their neighbour's work against the criteria as part of the learning process. The process of students correcting errors and embellishing what they have written *before* you collect it in for marking is not only beneficial to their learning but also makes it less likely that you will have to correct the same weaknesses over and over again in a range of work.

★ *Adopt a range of marking techniques*

To get away from working your way through a piece of written work and correcting every error, focus on particular aspects as you mark by ticking correct usage (e.g. a tense, word order) and underlining examples which are not right. Sometimes, I like to use highlighter pens as a quick and effective way of pinpointing for students what is good about their work and what needs to be improved; for example, you can highlight in green all the correct verbs or good parts, and in red the parts which are incorrect.

For more detailed correction, a school I know uses a checklist for errors, based on the sort of checklist which examination boards provide for GCSE written work. Each common error (e.g. wrong gender, wrong article, adjectival ending etc.) is numbered, and as they mark, teachers underline the error and write the number 'code' beside it. The school has a different version of the numbered error sheet for each Key Stage. This sort of approach works well as it gets students to reflect on their errors and put them right themselves. Another similar approach is to mark errors using symbols you have agreed within the department, for example, V means a verb formation error, T means a tense error and so on. Both approaches are preferable to you correcting every single error yourself.

If students email work to you for marking, you can mark it on screen and email it back to them if this is how you prefer to work. You need to make sure that the marking you are doing in this way is worthwhile and could not be done more effectively or efficiently in a more conventional way. As with any other marking, ensure that your students know the conventions you are using to show errors, so that the time you spend on the work leads to their acting on your feedback to improve their work.

Helping students to know how to improve through feedback

Giving effective feedback to students both orally and verbally is a key part of the assessment process.

★ *What makes effective feedback?*

Feedback to students is effective if it actually has an impact on their learning and work. Otherwise, it is a waste of time. Feedback can be given verbally or in writing through comments on work. You should aim to point out what is good about the students' work, and how they can improve it. Try to make your comments specific and your targets transferable to the next similar task they do. Make sure your comments are related to learning: continuous comments like 'underline your title' or 'make sure you use up all the pages in your book' take time to write but do not move the students' language learning on. Similarly, comments like 'Learn your spellings' or 'Improve your Spanish accent' are both too vague and too vast. It is better to pick out, for example, three specific common words which the student continuously misspells and ask him or her to learn these, or to specify one Spanish letter string or intonation feature which the student needs to work on.

If you use the target language to feed back to students on their work, you may find that your comments are less effective. I have seen many exercise books covered in 'Gut!' or 'Très bien!' Such comments are encouraging but do not show students how to improve. As with all target language issues, fitness for purpose is the key: will giving your comments in English lead to your students making more progress? If so, then use English. Of course, you can gradually build up your students' understanding of your comments so that they can ultimately understand and respond to comments in the target language: but if you are going to give them real high quality feedback of the type they get from their other subject teachers, the judicious use of English may well be required.

★ *Feeding back on listening and reading tasks*

Peer marking of listening and reading tasks provides the opportunity for students to get immediate feedback on their performance and to consider how they can improve.

On completion of tasks which students have marked in class, be sure to ask them to reflect on what they have learned from doing the task. Following a listening or reading task which you have marked together, for example, ask the class which questions caused them the most problems. Take a moment or two to talk through any difficult questions. I sometimes write keywords or phrases from a listening task on the board, or provide copies of the transcript, so that students can see in print what has caused them problems. In this way, students learn something from doing the task.

It is not easy to give students individual targets for how to improve their listening and reading skills. So following such a task get students to review their own performance and think about how they can improve. This helps students to reflect on techniques and strategies for improving their skills, for example, do they start off well and then lose concentration when it gets hard? Do they jump to conclusions instead of noticing, for example, negatives with a verb? You can get them to write down their target for next time they do a similar task.

★ *Feeding back on speaking tasks*

Feedback to students on their oral work is crucial and is often most easily given verbally. Try to briefly tell each student you listen to exactly what they have done well, and how they can improve. Such verbal feedback from you is highly effective but ephemeral. I like to get my students to record in their exercise book what I say to them so that they have a clear speaking target. They use a tick (√) and jot down beside it what I said was good, and a target (●) to note how I suggest they can improve.

> For example,   √   Nice *r* sound
>   ●   Adjectives AFTER noun

If you are listening to recordings of your students' work, use a similar approach to jot down for each student what is good and what can be improved. Be sure to feed back on different relevant areas, not just accuracy (see 'Feeding back on written work' section below.

★ *Feeding back on written work*

Giving effective feedback on written work is key to helping students know how to improve. Students tend to see accuracy as being the only measure of 'good' written work. However, students who find it difficult to be accurate can produce effective work in other ways, and through your comments, you can help them to see this.

Of course, your comments can focus on *accuracy*, for example:

- copying,
- tense use,
- accents,
- accurate verb forms/adjectival endings/etc.,
- punctuation,
- paragraphing,
- evidence of drafting/redrafting,
- spelling.

However, even from an early age, you can also focus on the *content* of the writing, for example:

- length,
- amount of information conveyed,
- imagination,
- extra details,
- humour,
- opinions,
- reasons for opinions,
- descriptions.

You can also focus on the *range and quality of language used,* for example:

- variety of vocabulary,
- variety of structures/tenses,
- use of unusual words,
- use of connectives,
- use of dictionary to find words of own,
- use of exercise book or resources for help,
- adaption of classwork,
- inclusion of complex sentences.

When you are writing targets for improvement on students' work, try to relate your targets back to the success criteria as well as giving students something to focus on which will apply next time they write a piece of work. To check that your target is a good one, ask yourself two questions:

1. Is it specific enough?
   and
2. Is it transferable to the next piece of written work they produce?

Here are some ideas for the sort of target you might write on a student's work:

- Use a greater range of vocabulary by using the dictionary to find words of your own.

- Vary your vocabulary by finding words you use twice and try to replace one of them with a synonym.
- Use relative pronouns to make your sentences more complex.
- Use each connective on the classroom list at least once in your piece.
- Include some negatives/past tense verbs/etc.
- Use your exercise book to find work done in class which will help.
- Include at least three adjectives whenever you describe something.
- Avoid starting sentences with *I*.
- Use pronouns other than *I* in your writing.
- Write at least (*five*) sentences.
- Give some more details (e.g. time, weather, who you were with, etc.).
- Include more opinions/reasons/questions etc.
- Say what you *don't* do, as well as what you do.
- Use the verb tables at the back of the book to help you get your (present tense) verbs more accurate.
- Divide your work up into paragraphs.
- Make a list of words you keep misspelling and check your work against this list.
- Read your work aloud to see if your punctuation seems correct.
- Highlight all your present tense verbs/adjectives/and the like and then go back and check if they seem correct.
- Check if each accent is *on* or *underneath* a letter.

(Copyright Suffolk CC, Providing Effective Feedback in MFL)

★ *Allow students time to respond to your feedback*

Set time aside in the lesson to enable students to read, consider and respond to your marking and feedback. Do not think this is a waste of class time as you have taken a good amount of your own valuable time to mark those books and write your comments.

You might ask your students to write out corrections for things you have highlighted or pointed out. As they are doing this, you can circulate and answer questions to clarify your corrections and comments. You could also ask students to rewrite the first couple of sentences or the last paragraph of their work, incorporating the advice you have given them in your comment.

When I return extended written work to students, or indeed extended speaking work which has been commented upon, I get them to use the back page of their exercise book to record their targets. They note down the date and copy out the short target I have given them. Before their next piece of work, they need to look back at the comment from last time and tick it off to show that they have tried to act upon it in this new piece. It is also easy for me to check on my previous target when I mark their next piece. Another good tip is to get students to copy their target from last time as a heading for their next piece of written work. This helps them to remember to focus on their target and means that you can easily refer to the target you set last time to see if the student has improved. Post-16 students can be encouraged to maintain an error log, recording key errors and noting when they have eradicated them for their work.

Other everyday classroom assessment techniques

★ Questioning

Modern languages teachers ask plenty of questions in their lessons. Here, we are talking about using questions to assess and develop students' understanding of key concepts and skills. This entails asking questions based not just on recall or comprehension of the language, but which probe students' thinking to see how much they actually understand.

The categories of Blooms' Taxonomy (see Chapter 8) help you structure the most effective type of questions to probe students' understanding, for example:

- Can you explain why . . .? *For example, Can you explain why this paragraph is better than that one?*
- Can you predict what will happen if . . .? *For example, Can you predict what will happen if I change 'he' to 'they' in this sentence?*
- Can you work out why . . .? *For example, Can you work out why these verbs are different from the others?*
- Can you use what you have learned to . . .? *For example, Can you use the structures you have learned from the article to write an email?*
- Can you evaluate . . .? *For example, Can you say which school system you think is better and why?*

You can ask questions like this to the whole class or to individuals as they are working. Black and Wiliams' work on assessment for learning has inspired lots of ideas for involving everyone in whole class question and answer sessions. Modern languages teachers can:

- allow 'thinking time' in pairs so that students have the chance to discuss answers together;
- use mini-whiteboards or other visual techniques so that everyone is required to give an answer;
- get students to build on each others' answers instead of you intervening each time;
- use 'no hands up' so that everybody is required to contribute;
- use 'phone a friend' so that students who are stuck can ask somebody else in the class to help them out.

As ever in modern languages, the question of target language use crops up. If the use of English for such questioning will help you both assess students' understanding and push their learning on, then you have a clear rationale for doing so.

★   *Peer and self-assessment*

Tips for successful peer and self-assessment include the following:

Make sure the criteria are clear

Do not just expect students to understand National Curriculum or examination board criteria as they appear in official documentation. If necessary, simplify the criteria into 'student speak'. For specific tasks, develop your own criteria from the generic levels or grade criteria so that students see how these apply to this piece of work.

Give students practice in evaluating work according to criteria

A good starter activity is to take an extract of written or spoken work and get students to work in pairs to grade it against the relevant criteria, explaining why. You can use work from past students (anonymized). You can also give students criteria for a specific grade or level and get them to produce an answer at that level.

Give students practice in giving feedback

Model to students what effective feedback looks like. You may like to ask them to give three positive comments and one point for improvement, for example. Use anonymous extracts and then get students to compare the comments they have made and how effective they are.

Vary your approach to peer assessment

- Ask students to swap books and assess their neighbour's work.
- Collect in the work and distribute out at random, then get students to assess the work they have been given.
- Get students to feed back after an oral presentation on what was good and what could be improved.
- Divide up aspects of the criteria across the class/group so that one person evaluates each aspect.

★ *Plenaries*

Plenaries at the end of or during the lesson make it easier for you to informally assess students' progress and understanding. Chapter 2 outlines ideas for plenary activities.

Reporting to parents

★ *Report writing*

The principles for providing effective feedback apply to report writing too. Make sure you know what the school's requirements are and keep to these. Aim to be specific in your comments. Start with what a student is good at and be positive about what he or she can do. Then say what the student needs to work on to improve further but avoid using jargon which parents are unlikely to understand. You will often be able to point to one of the four skills, grammatical understanding or vocabulary building as an area for improvement. If you are using banks of comments, make sure you personalize what you write for each student as students are very disgruntled to find their report to be exactly the same as their friend's.

★ *Parents' evenings*

The key to successful parents' evenings is to be prepared. I like to make a short note about each student so that I know what I am going to say. Take along your mark book or laptop so that you can refer to marks if necessary, but remember you have a very tight schedule and it is important to keep to time. Before the parents' evening, think about what you can suggest to parents to help their child improve, for example:

- Parents can help students learn vocabulary by testing them: even if parents do not know the language, they can say the English word and get the child to say and/or spell out the target language word.

- Make parents aware of the resources you have given their child which they can use at home (e.g. textbooks, vocabulary booklets or sheets, grammar notes).
- Make sure parents know about the support available to students through your school's virtual learning environment and any clubs or open sessions your department runs.
- Make parents aware of the best free websites which can be used for home practice by students.
- Extra resources can be purchased or borrowed (if appropriate to your school's situation), for example, a dictionary for home use, language magazines.

Making language learning real

Learning another language is more than studying another school subject: it is a gateway to a whole different world. Bringing the world of the target language country into your teaching will enhance your work and make language learning more memorable and real for your students.

Working with a Foreign Language Assistant (FLA)

★ The FLA scheme

Every year, a cohort of foreign students come to the United Kingdom to work as FLAs in British schools through the scheme organized by the British Council. If you are lucky enough to have an FLA working in your school, you have a living example of the target language and culture on tap! Some schools employ native speakers who live locally to work with learners. FLAs employed through the British Council are usually university students and therefore should have the advantage of being in tune with the latest aspects of youth culture and the ability to relate to your learners in a more informal way than you do as their teacher. Your FLA can also play a role in keeping you as a teacher up to date both linguistically and culturally, as well as providing authentic resources to help bring your subject alive.

★ *Organizing the work of the FLA*

FLAs in the United Kingdom are contracted to work for 12 hours a week, although this can be extended through agreement with individual FLAs. These 12 hours do not include preparation. Ensuring that this time is used fruitfully often means that FLAs work mostly with examination classes. FLAs are not employed to teach whole classes on their own and there must always be a teacher present if they are working with a whole class. Make sure that their timetable is clear and includes the name of the teacher and the room for each teaching group. If the FLA is to make a valuable contribution to your students' learning, it is absolutely vital that you tell the FLA what you would like them to do and prepare in advance of the lesson.

If the FLA's working hours do not allow him or her to work with the same class every week, it can be better to timetable the FLA to work with a class for a block of time, then switch to another class for the next block. This is easier for teachers to remember and plan for than if the FLA is timetabled with their class every fourth week, for example.

FLAs can work in different ways. With post-16 and older students, it is often most effective if the FLA works with small groups. In small-group situations, learners can really try out their language skills and have plenty of opportunities to speak and contribute. If you feel that younger students might misbehave in a small-group situation outside the classroom, incorporate the group work into your lesson, for example, as part of a carousel of activities within the classroom. FLAs can also work with the whole class with you present, and provide support for students as they work in the classroom on their speaking skills.

★ *What can the FLA do with your pupils?*

The FLA can, for example:

- practise general conversation questions and answers;

- practise a given set of structures;
- practise examination-type activities, such as talking about a picture with post-16 students;
- play board game–type activities with the students which require them to speak;
- give an illustrated talk and take questions on an aspect of culture (e.g. the school system, a favourite film);
- take on a role and answer questions prepared by the students (e.g. a farmer in the developing world, a hotel receptionist);
- present a song, poem or short extract from the target language culture and discuss it with students;
- use authentic materials to instigate discussion, comparisons and contrasts;
- model presentations for students and help them to produce their own.

The British Council website has a dedicated area with a great deal of help and advice for both schools and FLAs on how they can work best.

★ *Ensuring that the FLA has a good impact on learning*

When the FLA arrives, the head of department should give him or her a couple of weeks to observe teachers working in the classroom. During that time, ask the FLA to concentrate on two main things: first, how you use the target language in the classroom, especially what kind of language you choose to use and how you support this so that students understand; and second, how you build up students' confidence to contribute and speak. Even with a small group of post-16 students, allow the FLA time to observe so that he or she can see exactly what should be expected of your students and what they are able to do and understand.

Make sure that the FLA is focusing on building students' confidence and capability in speaking. There is likely to be little point in asking him or her to work with a group on a translation.

Your FLA may well be helping students prepare for examinations, but does he or she know what the examiner is looking for? Make sure your FLA has a copy of the oral criteria for your examination specification and that he or she understands what the criteria mean in practice. Sometimes, an FLA may focus too much on accuracy, which results in a loss of confidence on the student's part: sharing the assessment criteria with your FLA will help him or her to focus on all aspects of a student's performance.

Your FLA will be working with some students on a regular basis. Encourage him or her to get to know the students' names, for example, by using a seating plan, name stickers or Post Its© on the desk in front of each student. Whenever appropriate, ask the FLA to give students feedback on their performance, so that they have a concrete target to work on following their session. Structure the FLA's feedback for him or her by suggesting the use of a target sheet: the FLA tells students what they have done well and how to improve, and each student notes this down.

★ *Raising the profile of languages within the school*

By getting involved in other aspects of school life, the FLA can not only improve his or her own year abroad but also enrich the life of the school. If you have a modern languages team base or office where you all tend to congregate, encourage the FLA to go to the main staffroom so that he or she meets other members of staff from different areas of the school. If the FLA gets involved with sporting clubs, creative activities and trips and visits outside the modern languages department, colleagues and other students get the chance to learn about another culture and see for themselves what language learning can do for a young person.

Your FLA can organize and run a language club at lunchtimes or after school and organize competitions and quizzes. If your FLA is sufficiently confident, he or she can organize or contribute to school assemblies, or work with students on preparing a dance, drama or singing performance for the rest of the school.

Organizing successful trips, visits and exchanges

Visiting the target language country is a great way of getting students to see their language learning in a real context. They have the opportunity to use what they have learned in an authentic situation and experience the target language culture for themselves.

Sometimes, large modern languages departments find themselves functioning as travel agents! Be sure that your prime focus on a day-to-day basis is on learning and teaching in the classroom: this is what has the biggest impact on students. Do not undertake to lead a trip before you have built up some experience accompanying students on several trips led by somebody else. Make sure that you have sufficient administrative support for any visits which you are organizing so that you are not bogged down by sorting out finances and details. If you are leading a trip, make sure that you are in close liaison with the person in school who is in charge of trips and visits: he or she will know exactly what is required in terms of risk assessments, insurance and other legalities.

★ *Trips and visits to the target language country*

Students often feel most comfortable about going on a visit to the target language country with a group of fellow students and some familiar teachers. Such trips can be planned independently or you can use one of the many travel companies that offer a bespoke service to schools. Post-16 and older students can be involved in the organization of the trip, undertaking jobs like investigating websites and booking accommodation.

In order for students to get the best out of such a trip, you can prepare:

- A visit to an attraction or factory where students will hear the language spoken and meet people who live and work in the country.
- Some activities for students to do in the target language when they visit a specific town or village (e.g. a town trail with questions, a quiz).
- An oral activity (e.g. a survey for students to carry out with passers-by, provided this meets your school's safety guidelines; a question and answer session with the owner of your hotel or centre).
- A 'buying' task (e.g. groups of students need to purchase a given item for the packed lunch; students are given the task of negotiating with the hotel owner about an aspect of the trip).
- A written activity such as a diary or questionnaire which students complete on a daily basis.
- An ongoing vocabulary-gathering exercise (through a notebook or electronically) so that students are required to record at least a set number of new vocabulary items per day.
- Target language song sheets and bingo games for whiling away long journeys: if you are travelling by coach, use the bus microphone to lead the singing and activities.

Some travel companies offer ready-made teaching resources which are prepared by language teachers and therefore help you minimize your workload.

★ Exchange visits

Of all trips and visits, exchange visits have potentially the most value for students. Once our students leave school, it is unlikely that most of them will ever again have the chance to live with and be part of a family in another country. For many adults, the exchange visit experience, if they were lucky enough to have one, is still a vivid part of their memories of school.

In spite of this, exchange visits are declining in popularity. Students have become less confident about staying with another family. Parents, thanks in part to the increased emphasis on child protection issues, have become more reluctant to allow their offspring to stay with strangers. There have also been issues around checking UK families who are willing to host their child's partner in their own home.

Nevertheless, the exchange visit is still going strong in many schools and in some schools has been part of school life for several decades. Your school's policy on trips and visits will help you ensure that your exchange keeps your students safe while allowing them the chance to experience life from a foreigner's point of view.

A potential way of recruiting more students is to explore the possibility of linking up with another department within the school. Combining a linguistic exchange with a history trip or football tour can really increase your numbers as well as give students an even richer experience.

If you wish to set up a new exchange, personal contact is often a good starting point. Perhaps you have links with a school abroad, thanks to a year as an FLA or through family, colleagues or friends. Your FLA might have links which you can exploit. Otherwise, the British Council website provides helpful information and links.

When considering setting up a new exchange, a planning visit is vital, particularly if you do not know the school and the staff. Your school's headteacher should be able to facilitate this on the grounds of health and safety. During the visit, get to know the area, the school and the staff as well as you can. Discuss the information you need to match students up successfully and how you will share this. Raise any concerns you have now, as talking them through face to face will help to alleviate any problems later. Also, discuss timings for the visits and the potential programme, agreeing how much time will be spent in school, how much with partners and how much on excursions just for you and your students.

During the exchange, prepare some specific tasks for your students to do (see above for ideas). Some tasks, for example interviewing an adult family member about their likes/dislikes, the punctuation changes the emaning of this sentence can serve as useful icebreakers for getting your students to try out their target language.

★ *Work experience abroad*

Post-16 students or students studying for a vocational qualification will greatly benefit from a short period of time spent working in the target language country. Many teachers find it most practical to work with one of the commercial organizations that organize such experiences for UK students. You can also set this up for students yourself but, as usual, the legalities and safe-guarding issues need careful handling.

★ *Trips and visits in the United Kingdom*

Visits to the target language country are expensive and some families will not be able to afford to participate. Broaden your students' cultural horizons by ensuring that you arrange a trip to any local events which are culturally relevant. If your local cinema is showing a film in the language you are teaching, offer your students the chance to go along. Playwrights such as Molière and Brecht are often performed in local theatres: even if the play is performed in English, older and post-16 pupils in particular will benefit from seeing it on stage and there is always the opportunity to do some linked work back in the classroom. Music or dance groups from the target language country can also inspire your students: joint visits with another department in the school will help to increase your numbers. Visits to local industries where languages are used (see below) can also be motivating for students.

Engaging with the world through new technologies

Engaging with native speakers and visiting the target language country certainly make the world of the foreign language more real for students. Such contacts are not always possible on a day-to-day basis, however. New technologies enable students to engage with the whole world from the comfort of their own chairs. The familiarity with technology which young people have and how they use it on a daily basis needs to be exploited to show our students that languages are for real purposes. The motivational factor in using new technologies can be huge; as language teachers know, the motivation and the desire to communicate is half the battle when teaching languages.

Of course, digital technology is changing all the time. Consider becoming part of the modern languages teaching community which communicates regularly through Twitter and blogging: experts like Joe Dale and Alex Blagona are excellent people to follow as a starting point. In this way, you will keep up to date with how other teachers are constantly developing new and exciting ways of using technology in their modern languages lessons.

★ *Using web-based information sources to bring language learning alive*

Thanks to the web, there is a wealth and variety of texts from throughout the world, both written and aural, at our fingertips. Sifting through the sheer volume of material available to prepare the way for your students can take up far too much of your time. Students learn how to use data and information sources successfully at an early stage in their ICT learning: make use of these skills by making your tasks structured but open ended so that students need to decide for themselves where to find the information they need and evaluate their sources.

I like to provide a structured template or set of generic questions for students to use. In groups or pairs, they then have the freedom to explore cyberspace to find what they need. Your school should have filtered the internet to ensure that younger students do not access inappropriate sites.

Examples include using the internet to gather information about:

- a town or city in the target language country,
- a specific school,
- a specific business and how it functions,
- a specific shop and what is on sale there,
- specific leisure facilities,
- an environmental issue,
- critical views of a book, film or poem,
- a news story,
- a famous person,
- a custom or festival in the target language country,
- a cultural aspect of the target language country (e.g. cinema, pop music, the press).

What happens when students encounter texts which are too difficult and language they do not know because they have accessed material which is too complex for their current level of language? This is when you need to ask them to reflect on what their aim is, and draw their attention back to the questions you have set. What information do they actually need? Can they look for another site which will give them information in a more straightforward way? In this way, you are helping them to build up their analytical and evaluative skills at the same time as their linguistic skills as they learn to make choices about what is relevant to them and what is not. They can also discover for themselves the usefulness and limitations of tools such as online translators.

Using ICT in this way is a rich source of independent vocabulary acquisition as well. As part of the task set to students, it is a good idea to challenge them to find and record a fixed number of new words they have come across during their internet research.

★ *Making links with real native speakers*

Email links with classes abroad mean that information can be quickly and easily shared between students. When you are setting up an email link, a personal contact is often the best starting point. Other potential sources of partnerships are websites such as www.etwinning.net (for schools in Europe), or www.epals.com, which has a range of schools and classes from around the world which are looking for email partners and is a particularly good source of links outside Europe.

Class-based links are best based on specific areas or themes, with the timing of correspondence agreed in advance: you may not want to keep up an ongoing day-to-day conversation with the partner class but simply collaborate together once or twice a term.

The website www.epals.com suggests some creative collaborative tasks which classes might like to undertake together. On a simple level, you could exchange:

- Information about the students in your respective classes, for example, concerning themselves/their leisure activities/their homes/their holiday plans.
- Information or opinions about an area of culture, for example, the school system/TV programmes/energy-saving measures in the home.
- Data gathered through surveys or questionnaires and compare this with the email partner school's data.
- News from the local area or country.
- Opinions about global personalities, music, cinema or news stories.

Getting individual students to link up together in a safe way can be tricky if you have a big class. It can be more effective to use email links on a class basis and send emails as a class to each other rather than as individuals. You can compose and read emails together using the projector and screen. Students can also compose individual written texts and these can be joined together into one message.

The exchange of audio or visual material is another rich vein to be explored. Any oral activity (e.g. oral presentations, photo-based stories, sketches, songs, mock TV shows) can be recorded or filmed and sent to the partner school. Sometimes, students can be intimidated when they see that the level of language of their peers in the partner class seems higher than their own. Make sure that anything you send has been practised and improved. This is a particularly good time to focus on the importance of good pronunciation. Sometimes, it is appropriate for each school to send something in its native language; for example, you might choose to exchange typical children's songs, a poem studied by older students as part of their native tongue literature course or a piece of creative writing on a common theme.

Within your school's guidelines, post-16 students can get involved with discussions on forums, Facebook groups and other social media. They can read and leave target language comments on sites such as YouTube. The website www.flikr.com is a photo-sharing site where post-16 students can be encouraged to comment on and respond to photos taken by others. For example, during the 2010 Chilean mine crisis, a group of Spanish A-level students from an enterprising school in my area carried out a text-based dialogue in Spanish with a photographer at the scene in Chile, thanks to photos of the accident scene which the photographer had uploaded onto the *Flikr* website.

★ *Exploiting the worldwide audience*

Having a real audience and purpose for their work can be tremendously motivating for students, and the internet provides this. Use an area of the school's website or virtual learning environment (VLE) as a virtual 'gallery' where examples of students' work can be posted for others to see and comment upon. Similarly, if you set a particular task for students to do, the outcomes can be posted onto your blog or VLE so that students can read each others' work and borrow ideas from each other. This is particularly successful with post-16 students.

A school or class modern languages blog in the foreign language can encourage students to write regularly, concisely and for a purpose. With post-16 students, for example, a controversial question (e.g. is marriage still important nowadays?) can be posted through your blog and students asked to respond as part of their ongoing work. Through liaising with colleagues in your area, you could get students from other institutions to respond to the opinions expressed. You can ask the FLA, colleagues and friends from the target language country to add their thoughts to the blog. Sometimes, comments appear from people across the world who have engaged with the blog, which is very motivating for your students.

Making languages real through the world of work

★ *Setting up industry links*

Your school may well already have one or several links with existing local businesses. Find this information out from the member of staff in your school in charge of work-related learning, then contact the local businesses in question to find out if they have any staff who use a foreign language in their work. Even if the language used is not the language taught, students can still increase their awareness of the importance of languages in their locality.

CILT has some very useful information on its website regarding firms that have a real interest in promoting languages. The current 'Business Language Champions' scheme highlights firms that work with educational institutions to improve linguistic capability, and you will be able to find out about any local businesses that take part in this scheme. Your local Chamber of Commerce or Education and Business Partnership organization may well be able to provide you with other valuable contacts.

★   *Ways of working together*

Preparation is the key to working successfully with a local business. Business people are not teachers: you are. So if you are inviting a business person into your school or classroom, it is essential to arrange a planning meeting with him or her to discuss what he or she can offer, and how you can best exploit this expertise. Possibilities include the following:

Presentation at an options assembly or to a group of modern languages students

Agree time limits and plan together some element of interaction, for example, some questions with options for which students must vote by raising their hand. If your industry-link colleague is not used to addressing a group of young people, set the presentation up 'chat show' style with yourself (or an older student) as the interviewer.

Setting up a classroom task or activity

This can work very well if the task is based on a real one which the business actually requires. This might be designing an area of a website, for example, or producing product packaging for a specific audience.

Using materials provided by the business for classroom-based work

This could be the database which a local hotel chain uses for booking in clients; orders or invoices which are in the target language; or target language emails regarding the setting up of a meeting. Mundane tasks become hugely more engaging for students if they see that they really do relate to the outside world.

Visiting the company to find out how languages are used
This can be a straightforward tour with a talk. Even better is to involve students in some sort of authentic task while they are on-site. A school I know has been able to use the premises of its linked business as a setting for NVQ languages students to film role-play assessment scenarios.

References, further reading and useful websites

Adams, J. with Panter, S. A. (2001) *Just Write!* London: CILT.

Alison, J. and Halliwell, S. (2002) *Challenging Classes: Focus on Pupil Behaviour.* London: CILT.

Barton, A. (2004) *Getting the Buggers into Languages.* London: Continuum Press.

Black, P., Harrison, C., Lee, C., Marshall, B. and Wiliam, D. (2004) *Working Inside the Black Box: Assessment for Learning in the Classroom.* London: NFER Nelson.

Black, P. and Wiliam, D. (1998) *Inside the Black Box.* London: NFER Nelson.

Coyle, D., Holmes, B. and King, L. (2009) *Towards an Integrated Curriculum: CLIL National Statement and Guidelines.* London: The Languages Company.

Jones, B. (2001) *Developing Learning Strategies.* London: CILT.

Jones, B. and Jones, G. (2001) *Boys' Performance in Modern Foreign Languages: Listening to Learners.* London: CILT.

Jones, J. and Wiliam, D. (2008) *Modern Foreign Languages Inside the Black Box.* London: GL Assessment.

McLachlan, A. (2001) *Advancing Oral Skills.* London: CILT.

OFSTED (2011) *Modern Languages: Achievement and Challenge 2007–2010.* London: OFSTED.

Pillette, M. (2005) *L'Oreille Fine* (www.challengingideas.co.uk/MartinePillette.htm).

Rendall, H. (2001) *Stimulating Grammatical Awareness: A Fresh Look at Language Acquisition.* London: CILT.

Shaw, G. (ed.) (2000) *Aiming High 2.* London: CILT.

Swarbrick, A. (ed.) (1994) *Teaching Modern Languages.* London: Routledge.

Useful teaching resources

Authentik Magazines (www.authentik.ie/).
Key Stage 2 Framework for Languages (DCFS publication, available at www.primarylanguages.org.uk).
Mary Glasgow Magazines (http://maryglasgowplus.com/).
Pedagogy and Practice: Teaching and Learning in Secondary Schools (DCSF publication, available through the National Archives website).
Training Materials for the Foundation Subjects (DCSF publication, available through the National Archives website).

Useful websites

★ *General websites*

www.all-languages.org.uk: The Association for Language Learning represents teachers of all languages in the United Kingdom.
www.cilt.org.uk: CILT (formerly the National Centre for Languages, now part of CfBT Education Trust) offers a wealth of information on all aspects of language teaching in the United Kingdom.
www.languageswork.org.uk: This contains information, ideas and resources about languages and the world of work, including sections for career advisers and materials for classroom use.
www.bfi.org.uk: The British Film Institute's education pages include ideas on how to use film in the modern languages classroom.
www.britishcouncil.org: Includes information on opportunities abroad, linking opportunities and the Foreign Language Assistant scheme.
www.etwinning.net: A site for linking with other schools in Europe.
www.epals.com: A site for setting up links with schools all over the world.

★ *Examination board websites*

England
www.aqa.org.uk
www.edexcel.com
www.ocr.org.uk

Wales
www.wjec.co.uk

Scotland
www.sqa.org.uk/

Northern Ireland
www.rewardinglearning.org.uk (CCEA website)

★ *Sample resource-sharing websites*

www.sunderlandschools.org/mfl-sunderland/
www.mflresources.org.uk/
www.tes.co.uk/teaching-resources/
www.languagesresources.co.uk/
www.lerndeutsch.org.uk

★ *Some current modern languages teacher blogs*

Alex Blagona: http://alexblagona.blogspot.com/
Chris Fuller: http://chrisfuller.typepad.com/
Joe Dale: http://joedale.typepad.com/
Rachel Hawkes: http://rachelhawkes.typepad.com/

★ *Examples of commercial travel operators*

www.halsbury.com/www.nstgroup.co.uk/
www.ststravel.co.uk
www.workexperienceabroad.co.uk

Index